THE MAN IN THE IRON MASK

The man in the iron mask is no legend. Myths and stories have grown up around his person, many deliberately spread to mislead the inquisitive: but such a person really existed, shut away on the direct orders of the king.

Here was a man who knew something so important, so incredible, that if he opened his mouth to try and tell his secret, his guards had orders to run him through with their swords. Two of the ministers detailed to secure him were almost certainly murdered when the king felt that they could no longer be trusted. Why was someone so dangerous being kept alive? Why had he not been killed at the start?

Here was a man whose face must be forever concealed from the public gaze, even though he was securely locked up, even though the key to his cell was kept in the pocket of the safest gaoler in France. Why? Who would recognise him after a third of a century? Who was he that he could be so easily recognised? Or was his face disfigured, so hideously scarred that no-one could bring themselves to look? And why, for so many years, did he remain resigned to his fate, without tears or tantrums, without even once trying to escape? What awful event had overtaken his life that made it impossible for him to return? Or were the consequences of trying to escape simply too dreadful to contemplate?

About the author

Harry Thompson is a Senior Producer at Radio 4, working in the light entertainment area. He has written for *Private Eye*, the *Listener* and the *Independent*, as well as for *Spitting Image Productions* and *Not the Nine O'Clock News* on TV.

The Man in the Iron Mask

Harry Thompson

NEW ENGLISH LIBRARY
Hodder and Stoughton

Copyright © Harry Thompson
1987

First published in Great Britain in
1987 by George Weidenfeld &
Nicolson Limited

New English Library Paperback
Edition 1990

The publishers are grateful to the
following for permission to use
illustrations:
Archives Photographiques, BBC
Hulton Picture Library, Collection
Viollet, Maurice Gaulmin and The
Mansell Collection

Printed and bound in Great Britain
for Hodder and Stoughton Paper-
backs, a division of Hodder and
Stoughton Ltd., Mill Road,
Dunton Green, Sevenoaks, Kent
TN13 2YA. (Editorial Office: 47
Bedford Square, London
WC1B 3DP) by Clays Ltd., St Ives
plc, Bungay, Suffolk.

British Library C.I.P.
Thompson, Harry
   The man in the iron mask
   1. France. Man in the Iron Mask
   I. Title

   ISBN 0-450-53721-8

Contents

To Roy Davies

The family tree of the royal families of England and France

insofar as it concerns the events related in this book

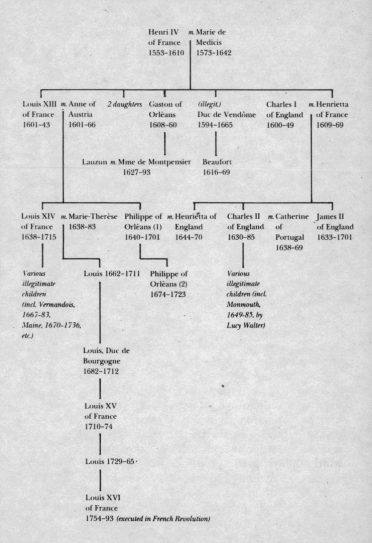

Henri IV *m.* Marie de
of France   Medicis
1553–1610   1573–1642

Louis XIII *m.* Anne of   *2 daughters*   Gaston of   *(illegit.)*   Charles I *m.* Henrietta
of France   Austria   Orlèans   Duc de Vendôme   of England   of France
1601–43   1601–66   1608–60   1594–1665   1600–49   1609–69

Lauzun *m.* Mme de Montpensier   Beaufort
            1627–93   1616–69

Louis XIV *m.* Marie-Therèse   Philippe of *m.* Henrietta of   Charles II *m.* Catherine   James II
of France   1638–83   Orlèans (1)   England   of England   of   of England
1638–1715   1640–1701   1644–70   1630–85   Portugal   1633–1701
                                                                              1638–69

Various   Louis 1662–1711   Philippe of   *Various*
illegitimate   Orlèans (2)   *illegitimate*
children   1674–1723   *children (incl.*
(incl. Vermandois,   *Monmouth,*
1667–83,   *1649-85, by*
Maine, 1670–1736,   *Lucy Walter)*
etc.)

Louis, Duc de
Bourgogne
1682–1712

Louis XV
of France
1710–74

Louis 1729–65

Louis XVI
of France
1754–93 *(executed in French Revolution)*

1

Introducing the iron mask

One chilly afternoon towards the end of November in the year 1703, two men stood in the Paris churchyard of St Paul. They had come to bury their dead. No others were there to witness the undistinguished coffin being lowered into its freshly dug grave; only a tiny handful of people even knew that the funeral was taking place. The two men hurried unceremoniously through the little service and headed back for the church, a great weight lifted from their minds.

The man they had buried was one of the most important of his time, but nobody mourned his passing. Nobody knew his name, because he didn't have one any more. And nobody could have recognised his face, because if they had lifted the lid off the coffin they would have seen that he no longer had a face. His features had been destroyed.

Some miles to the south of the city, in his opulent palace at Versailles, the news was carried to the king. That day, like every other day at Versailles, was a continuous, overweight circus of entertainment revolving around the royal personage. Louis XIV, the 'Sun King', whose reign was the most glorious in history, lived his daily life in a whirl of plays, parties, concerts and banquets, while fawning courtiers admired him in everything he did. But today was different. For thirty-four years a nagging fear had underpinned all the jollity, a fear of one faceless, nameless prisoner locked in a cell and what might happen if he were to escape. Today that fear was finally lifted, and the revels could go in earnest.

The man in the iron mask is no legend. Myths and stories have grown up around his person, many deliberately spread to mislead the inquisitive; but such a person really existed, shut away on the direct orders of the king. And great battlements, triple doors, iron bars and whole brigades of soldiers made sure that he stayed there until the day he died.

To this day – in a sense – he has not been released from his prison, because nobody has unravelled the mystery. Many have tried, among them famous names such as Voltaire and Alexandre Dumas, but for the most part only a few novels and some tortuous and unlikely stabs at a solution have resulted from three centuries of detective work. Yet here was a man whose secret and whose identity were of such enormous importance that he was kept locked in solitary confinement, his face covered, for a third of a century. Not for him the rat-infested dungeon of the common criminal: this was a man of considerable importance, maintained at a cost of millions, while the peasant families of France struggled on the equivalent of £10 a week. But no-one of any consequence had disappeared.

Here was a man who knew something so important, so incredible, that if he opened his mouth to try and tell his secret, his guards had orders to run him through with their swords. Two of the ministers detailed to secure him were almost certainly murdered when the king felt that they could no longer be trusted. Why was someone so dangerous being kept alive? Why had he not been killed at the start?

Here was a man whose face must be forever concealed from the public gaze, even though he was securely locked up, even though the key to his cell was kept in the pocket of the safest gaoler in France. Why? Who would recognise him after a third of a century? Who was he that he could be so easily recognised? Or was his face disfigured, so hideously scarred that no-one could bring themselves to look? And why, for so many years, did he remain resigned to his fate, without tears or tantrums, without even once trying to escape? What awful event had overtaken his life that made it impossible for him to return? Or were the consequences of trying to escape simply too dreadful to contemplate?

Not only are we dealing with one of the most famous unresolved mysteries of all time, but we have before us a 'whodunnit' without a crime or a motive. Only a punishment of astonishing and theatrical severity remains to tantalise us. Neither is it simply a question of marshalling the facts and laying them end to end: for in this investigation we are dealing with an adversary. Here, we find a page ripped from the records; there, a false rumour planted, to lead the unwary investigator astray. These obstacles and false clues are the marks of deception laid down by no less a saboteur than the Sun King himself.

Why did Louis xiv, the most powerful man in Europe, a king who would afford no more than a few minutes of his time to the most important nobles in France, live in fear of one silent, faceless, nameless man, shut away in a prison cell, a man whom he felt compelled to keep alive? What was the unknown bond that drew the king to his mysterious prisoner?

To this day, nobody has produced a solution that satisfactorily answers all these questions, and the many others raised by the mystery. This book aims to provide that solution: but here you will find all the evidence, including the misleading and the incorrect, and all the other theories that have been advanced on the subject, to enable you to judge correctly for yourself. It is a story that brings together Napoleon, Cyrano de Bergerac and the Three Musketeers, that unites kings and queens with concubines and conmen, that espouses espionage, blackmail, kidnapping, poison and black magic. It is also a story that requires careful historical consideration, because some famous reputations are at stake.

2

Death of a nameless prisoner

Neither Major Rosarges nor Doctor Reilhe, the two men who supervised the burial of the masked man, had any real idea of the true identity or importance of their illustrious corpse. For the doctor, it was a simple matter of signing a false name on the death certificate and bowing out of the conspiracy, secure in his ignorance. But the major must have been consumed by his curiosity. A soldier in name only, he had been a prison warder for thirty-four years: his life had revolved around his captive. The job had brought him success and riches, but he was absolutely forbidden to ask the prisoner the simplest of questions. Even after the masked man's death he was expected to take part in the cover-up, and put his name to the 'official version' of the burial contained in the parish register.

The church and cemetery of St Paul were destroyed in the 1790s, and today the bones of the dead lie jumbled and buried below the modern streets of Paris, forever out of reach; so the major and the doctor's entry in the register is the only surviving record of the burial. It is deliberately vague. It identifies the time, the place and the participants of the dubious ceremony, but otherwise it is of little use. It is a document that must be treated with caution, for like the burial it was meant to mislead the inquisitive. It reads:

On the 19th, Marchioly, aged 45 or thereabouts, died at the Bastille, whose body was buried in the cemetery of St

Paul, his parish, the 20th of the present month, in the presence of M. Rosage, the Major of the Bastille, and of M. Reglhe[1], surgeon of the Bastille, who signed, Rosarges, Reilhe.

But while you can destroy a man's face, and a man's name, you cannot destroy a memory. Long after the 1703 burial, rumours had spread through the Bastille about the life and death of the nameless prisoner. Father Griffet, who came to the fortress as chaplain soon afterwards, told of the incredible secrecy surrounding his death:

The memory of the masked prisoner was still preserved among the Officers, the soldiers and the servants of the Bastille . . . and those who had seen him with his mask, when he passed them in the courtyard on his way to attend Mass, said that it was ordered after his death, to burn practically everything he had used, such as linen, clothes, mattresses, blankets etc., that even the walls of the room where he was lodged had to be scraped and whitewashed again, and that all the tiles of the flooring were taken up and replaced by others, so much did they fear that he had found the means to conceal some note or some mark, the discovery of which could have revealed his name.

Chevalier, the Major of the Bastille at a later date, confirmed the details of his death:

The famous man in the mask, whose identity was never known . . . was treated with great distinction by Monsieur the Governor and was only seen by Monsieur de Rosarges, Major of the said castle, who had this task alone; he was not at all ill, except for a few hours, and died rather suddenly. [He was] Interred at St Paul's on Tuesday, 20 November 1703 at four o'clock in the afternoon, under the name Marchierques:[2] he was buried in a new white shroud which was given by the Governor, and practically everything that was found in his room was burnt, such as his entire bed; and including mattresses, tables, chairs and other utensils, reduced to dust and cinders, and thrown into the latrines. The rest was melted down, like silver, copper, tin. This prisoner's room was scraped down to the heart of the stone, and whitewashed anew from top to bottom. The doors and the windows were burnt with the rest.

There was also a prisoner who described the masked man, called Linguet:

The Governor himself used to serve him and collect his laundry. When he went to Mass, he was most expressly forbidden to speak or show his face; the order had been given to the soldiers to fire at him [if he did]: their guns were certainly loaded with bullets; also he had to take great care to conceal himself and to be silent. When he was dead, everything was inspected and burnt.

Clearly, this was no ordinary prisoner. To begin with, he was being held in the Bastille. Captives in the Bastille were not chained to a wall in a rotting dungeon, but were usually fed on good food and wine, allowed fine furniture, musical instruments, games, even their own pets to keep them company. Some were political prisoners, often kept secure in the luxury to which they were accustomed. And this prisoner, we are told, was treated with 'great distinction' by the governor, St Mars, and Major Rosarges, the only two men permitted to see him. He ate his meals off silver plates. Indeed tradition holds that he was accorded every desire but the return of his liberty and his identity.

Already a picture is emerging of a prisoner who was treated with civility but who was strictly forbidden from communicating with the outside world; who soon after his death had already become the famous 'masked man'; and whose identity remained a secret even in death, right down to the falsifying of his death certificate, the desecration of his corpse and the destruction of his belongings. All these details confirm the immense importance that the authorities attached to this one man, but they provide no clues with which to proceed further. Indeed, the conspirators thought that they had made their secret watertight, for when King Louis XIV died in 1715 the world was still in complete ignorance about his mysterious masked prisoner. Prison rumours abounded about the man's lifestyle and his startling disguise but, frustratingly, no concrete clues existed that might explain who he was or where he had come from.

That is, until about fifty years later, when the journal of Etienne du Jonca was discovered. At the time of the masked man's imprisonment du Jonca was the king's lieutenant at the Bastille, officially second in command to the governor: he was a learned man with erudite connections, and it transpired that – fortunately for us – he had begun to keep a diary in 1690. Turning to the entry of November 1703, we find the following:

> On the same day, Sunday 19 November 1703, the unknown prisoner, always masked with a mask of black velvet, whom Monsieur de St Mars, the Governor, brought with him on coming from the Isle of Sainte-Marguerite, whom he had kept for a long time, he [the prisoner] finding himself to be somewhat ill yesterday on leaving Mass, died today, at about ten o'clock at night, without having had a serious illness; it could not have been slighter; Monsieur Giraut, our chaplain, confessed him yesterday. Surprised by death, he did not receive the sacraments, and our chaplain exhorted him a moment before he died. And this unknown prisoner, kept there for so long, was buried on Tuesday at 4 o'clock in the afternoon, on the 20 November, in the cemetery of St Paul, our parish: on the register of the burial he was given a name, also unknown. Monsieur de Rosarges, Major and Arreil, signed the register.

In the margin is added: 'I have since learned that they have called him Monsieur de Marchiel[3] on the register, and that forty pounds was paid for the funeral.'

Here at least are concrete clues, leads to follow up, and

du mesme Jour landy -19- me de
novembre 1703 — le prisonnier
Inconneu touiours masqué d'un masque
de velours noir que monsieur de
St mars gouuerneur a mené auec
luy en venant des isles St margue
quil gardoit depuis Contampts lequel
setant trouue hier un peu mal en
sortant dela messe il est mort
se Jourdhuy sur les dix heures du
soir sans auoir eu unne grande
maladie il ne se peut pas moins
mr giraut nostre aumonier le
confessa hier sur prié de la mort
il napoint receu les sacrements
et nostre aumonier la exorté un
momant auend que de mourir
et se prisonnier Inconneu garde de
puis silontampts a esté enterré
le mardy a quattre heures de la
apres midy -20- me novembre dan
le Cemetiere St paul nostre pa
de apres du voisse sur le registre moreuu
depuis contanct on a donné un nom aussy Incon
nome sur le registre que monsieur de vo saujes mais
one on apelle et un reil Kieurgien qui hom
Seruant Signe Sur le registre

Extract from the diary of Etienne du Jonca, November 1703

an interesting fact – that the prisoner apparently wore a mask not of iron, but of black velvet. Linguet confirmed this too: 'He wore a mask of velvet and not of iron, at least during the time that he spent at the Bastille'. For many years the earliest known reference to an iron mask came from Voltaire, although he later amended this to say that the mask only had a steel-reinforced chinpiece. In the last few years, though, a much earlier mention of a metal mask has been discovered, which will be debated at the end of this book. An iron mask purporting to be the original was exhibited in 1855, but nobody has been able to find out where this came from.

We are not yet finished with Etienne du Jonca. The prisoner, he says, arrived with the governor St Mars from the prison on the Isle of Sainte-Marguerite. Turning the pages of his journal back five years we find the confirmation of this:

> On Thursday, 18 September, at three o'clock in the afternoon, Monsieur de St Mars, Governor of the castle of the Bastille, made his first appearance, coming from his command of the Isles of Sainte-Marguerite and Saint-Honorat, bringing with him, in his litter, an ancient prisoner[4] that he had at Pignerol, whom he caused to be always masked, whose name is not mentioned; directly he got out of the carriage he put him in the first room of the Basinière Tower, waiting until night for me to take him, at 9 o'clock, and put him with M. de Rosarges, one of the sergeants that the Governor brought, alone in the third single room of the Bertaudière Tower, which I had furnished with all the necessaries some days before his arrival, having received orders to that effect from Monsieur de St Mars: in conducting him to the said room, I was accompanied by Sieur Rosarges ... who will be charged with serving and looking after the said prisoner, who will be maintained by the Governor.

It was an unusual arrival that had not escaped the notice of the newspaper. References in the *Gazette d'Amsterdam* at the time mentioned that:

Monsieur de St Mars, previously Governor of the islands of Saint-Honorat and Sainte-Marguerite, arrived several days ago, to take over the government of the Bastille, with which he has been entrusted by His Majesty . . . [he] has brought to it a prisoner whom he brought with him.

But nobody would have seen the masked prisoner being taken in or out. For when the carefully screened litter approached the great gates of the Bastille that September afternoon, in a well-rehearsed procedure, the guards closed all the shops clustered around the massive fortress, and turned their faces to the wall, not daring even to catch a glimpse of the king's personal prisoner.

Almost a hundred years later in 1789, the French revolutionaries smashed those walls to rubble and overthrew the Bourbon dynasty. With the Bastille thrown open, one of their first tasks was to set up a commission to investigate its secret archives, and settle once and for all the mystery of the masked man; but when the commission's leader, Charpentier, reported in 1790, it became clear that they had found hardly any new facts. Just two new items emerged. First, they found that the Marquis de Louvois, who was appointed minister for war (and therefore also for legal matters) in 1666, had been the first man to take charge of the secret; and secondly, they discovered a reference in an official letter of April 1691 to 'the prisoner who has been in custody for twenty years'.

In the wake of the revolution the archives of the Bastille were scattered and lost, and it seemed that no-one would be able to examine them again. Then, one day in 1840, a young assistant at the library of the Arsenal in Paris, named François Ravaisson, was repairing his kitchen. He lifted one of his floorboards, and to his amazement discovered great piles of yellowing documents. The missing archives were found, and Ravaisson dedicated his life to restoring and cataloguing them.

Among those Bastille archives is the castle's Great Register, a list of all its prisoners, and it is here that we can discover official confirmation of du Jonca's revelations. The masked man is given no name in the register, certainly not the false one applied to his death certificate. But it does state, in the column of prisoners' names:

> Ancient prisoner of Pignerol, always obliged to wear a mask of black velvet, of whom nothing has ever been known about his name or qualities.

In the column listing the crime for which each prisoner has been incarcerated, it simply says that 'It has never been known'. A much later addition confirms: 'This is the famous Man in the Mask, whom nobody has ever known.'

Unsurprisingly, the uncovering of the secret papers of the Bastille by the French revolutionaries had not revealed the one secret they had so desperately sought – the prisoner's real name. The document that Ravaisson later discovered, together with the journals of du Jonca, only confirmed the existence of the man in the mask, but did not seem to enlighten them any further.

Yet by analysing these guarded scraps of official jotting line by line, a solid body of information about our subject does begin to take shape. Already it has been established that he died on the 19 November 1703 and was buried under the name of 'Marchioly'. He had been imprisoned in great secrecy and comfort in the Bastille, initially in the third single room of the Bertaudière Tower, for five years. Whilst in the Bastille, his name and crime were unknown, and he was attended only by the governor and Major Rosarges. He was kept permanently masked in black velvet – presumably so that he would not be recognised. He was a Catholic: he attended mass, and was expected to receive confession and the sacraments at death. He was buried in a Catholic cemetery. He had arrived on the 18 September 1698, in the charge of the new governor, St Mars. He had always been the prisoner of St Mars, first at the fortress of Pignerol, and later on the Isles of Sainte-Marguerite. And he had been a prisoner since approximately 1671, but not before the appointment of Louvois as minister of war in 1666.

These last two are the most important clues: for they firmly identify two prisons that he had been held in, name the gaoler and the minister who had kept him there, and give us a rough date of his arrest – the late 1660s or early 1670s. These clues provide a useful start – but only a start. As yet we know only the barest facts. But for many years, amateur detectives had nothing more to go on; these facts were all that were known about 'the man in the iron mask'. They formed the basis for all the great theories about the mystery, including the most famous theory of all: the story of the Three Musketeers' last adventure.

Notes on Chapter 2

1 At this time, the spelling of names was rarely standardised.
2 Obviously a confused version of 'Marchioly'.
3 As with the church register, the spelling of names is not standardised.
4 The term 'ancient prisoner' verges on a nickname: but the implication contained in the original French is 'a prisoner of very long standing'.

3

The Musketeers' last stand

The story of how the Three Musketeers rescued the man in the iron mask from prison and installed him as the true king on the throne of France, only to have the position reversed and to meet their own destruction in the process, has come to be accepted in the popular imagination as the true story of the man in the iron mask. The success of Alexandre Dumas' novel has also led to a legendary status being conferred upon the mysterious prisoner, who of course was only too real. In fact Dumas used a clever mixture of fact and fiction in his stories – his unlikely yarn was spun upon a genuine historical frame.

In the Three Musketeers' last adventure, we find that – unknown to his friends – Musketeer Aramis has quietly become a bishop, and also General of the Jesuits at the same time, which is no mean feat. Somehow he has discovered the identity of the man in the iron mask into the bargain. The masked man, we are told, is a secret twin of King Louis xiv, born after his brother. At that time, the second-born of twins was commonly considered to be the elder, by virtue of being conceived first. First in, last out, as it were. But by the time this twin is born, brother Louis has already been proclaimed heir to the throne in error, so – to avoid any confusion – the hapless child is brought up in ignorance of his real status. Not long afterwards, he discovers his true identity by chance and is cast into prison, masked and silenced.

Aramis, cunning and unscrupulous in his old age, hatches a daring plot to switch the two brothers, the king and the wretched prisoner. This is because he hopes to save his great friend, the finance minister, Nicolas Fouquet, who is about to be indicted for embezzlement and corruption by the king. Alexandre Dumas made a hero out of Nicolas Fouquet, presenting him as generous, warm-hearted and misunderstood. In fact the real Fouquet, although a cultured and scholarly man, was notorious for the extent of his corruption. He built great palaces and threw enormous parties using the contents of the state coffers, and nearly bankrupted France in the process.

Dumas makes no attempt to explain where the 'misunderstood' Fouquet of his story gets his millions from. But Fouquet is vital to our investigation: for, with a clever historical touch, Dumas has chosen a man who was in fact imprisoned in the fortress of Pignerol from 1665 until his death – at the same time as the man in the mask. And in a true episode used by Dumas, Fouquet was actually arrested by the real d'Artagnan, who recommended none other than St Mars as the gaoler most likely to keep him securely shut away. Fouquet has even been put forward as a candidate for the mysterious prisoner, even though his death is well attested in 1680 at the age of 65. He is a character who will require further investigation.

The fictional Fouquet of Dumas' story proves too honourable to allow his former king to languish in gaol, and switches the two brothers back again, even though it means his own downfall. For the Musketeers, the end is inevitable. Pursued by the vengeful Louis to the furthest corner of France, the brave and loyal (but rather stupid) Porthos – still not really understanding what has happened to make him fall from grace – gives his own life to save Aramis, holding off the pursuing troops until his friend can get away.

Athos dies of grief soon after, and Aramis escapes to Spain: d'Artagnan remains in the royal service, but is killed in action soon after delivering Fouquet to his prison.

It is an epic, tragic and, to be honest, rather silly romance, but one that contains a good deal of interest. The theory that the man in the iron mask was an unwanted royal twin is a very important one. In fact Dumas got his story from two earlier investigators, Dorat-Cubières, writing in 1789, and the Abbot Soulavie, who wrote in 1790. Writing during the revolution, when anything anti-royal was well received, they claimed that a royal twin was born after the young Louis had already been proclaimed heir, and that the all-powerful Cardinal Richelieu persuaded the father, Louis XIII, to keep the fact a secret, lest it one day cause a civil war. The proof lay in a secret document supposedly written by the gaoler St Mars, and supposedly obtained by Mademoiselle de Valois by prostituting herself to the prince regent after Louis XIV's death. The document was found in the foreign ministry archives, but this means little, as the foreign ministry was used as a repository for all kinds of papers seized during the revolution. It reads:

The unhappy Prince whom I have brought up and whom I guarded to the end of his days, was born on the 5 September 1638, at half past eight in the evening, while the King was at supper. His brother, now reigning [Louis XIV], was born at twelve, his father being at dinner. The pomp and ceremony which attended the birth of the King contrasted with that of his brother which was wretched and carefully concealed. Louis XIII was warned from the Queen's chamber that Her Majesty was about to be delivered of a second child: and this double birth had already been predicted to him a long time previously by two shepherds, who had said in Paris that if the Queen was brought to bed of two Dauphins,[1] the state was lost. The Cardinal Richelieu, consulted by the King, replied that, 'If two children were born, the second must be carefully put out of sight, since he might one day claim the throne.' Tormented by uncertainty as to what course he should follow, the King's distress was overwhelming.

Soulavie goes on to tell of how, at the age of nineteen, the second twin discovers his identity and is immediately imprisoned. However, we can immediately destroy this theory by pointing to a number of historical inconsistencies that show the document to be forged. First, if St Mars had this kind of knowledge (which is unlikely) he would certainly have been forbidden from officially committing it to paper in any form – nor would he have dared to. Secondly, Cardinal Richelieu was at St Quentin on 5 September 1638, and did not return until 2 October, so he could not have been present at the birth. Thirdly, if the man in the mask was imprisoned at 19, that would put the date at 1657, nine years before the appointment of Louvois as minister and seven years before his gaoler St Mars took up office at Pignerol. Fourthly, there is absolutely no reason why Louis XIII would not have wanted twins – it is a ridiculous suggestion to say that he would have got rid of one of his own sons. He was desperate to secure the succession (as was Richelieu), indeed he would stop at nothing to prevent it falling to his brother Gaston d'Orléans, and in an age of high infant mortality he would have wanted as many children as possible. Fifthly, all royal babies were public events, taking place in front of at least twenty important court personages: any irregularities would have been easily spotted. And sixthly, why had Madamoiselle de Valois never publicised this supposed document herself, or indeed shown it to anybody at the time? The traditional theory of the man in the iron mask is easily discredited. But we have not returned all the way to square one: for Dumas' story and the sources that he drew it from, although now proved to be a forgery, raise two interesting and not unlikely possibilities. One, that the man in the mask was imprisoned because he looked like the king; and two, that the cunning Cardinal Richelieu may have organised the plot, for reasons we have yet to discover. We have not seen the last of the cardinal in this story.

We cannot dismiss this kind of evidence completely out of hand, because although the story had become the province of novelists and forgers only eighty years after the masked man's death, their material was based on a solid body of popular rumour: and underneath that rumour lies the truth.

Notes on Chapter 3

1 The name given to the heir to the French throne.

4

The first detective

The first detective to investigate the case of the man in the iron mask was the writer Voltaire. He spent some years trying to solve the mystery, and has done us a great service by collecting all the rumours circulating at the time, whether true or untrue, and trying to make sense of them. Voltaire himself was imprisoned in the Bastille for minor offences, in 1717 and 1726, and it was here that he first heard tell of the mysterious prisoner. On 30 October 1738 he wrote in a letter: 'I am fairly well informed on the adventure of the man in the iron mask who died at the Bastille. I have spoken to people who served him.'

Voltaire was a little too confident in the accuracy of his information, for as we now know, the mask he wore at the Bastille was made of black velvet. But whatever it was that Voltaire learnt in the prison made him keen to pursue the matter. He scoured France for information, visiting the Isles of Sainte-Marguerite, and questioning peasants along the route from there to the Bastille. In 1751, the results of his research were published.

Some years after the death of Mazarin[1], an event happened which was not to be paralleled, and, what is no less strange, is unnoticed by all the historians. An unknown prisoner, of unusual stature, young, of graceful and noble appearance, was sent in great secrecy to the Isle of Sainte-Marguerite in the sea of Provence. This

prisoner wore a mask on the road, the chin of which had
steel springs, which allowed him the freedom to eat with
his mask on. Orders were given to kill him if he
uncovered himself. He remained on the island until a
trusted officer, named St Mars, Governor of Pignerol,
was made Governor of the Bastille in 1690. He went to
the Isle of Sainte-Marguerite and brought him to the
Bastille with his mask on all the way. The Marquis de
Louvois went to see him on that island before his
departure, and spoke to him, without sitting down, in a
manner which showed great respect. This stranger was
brought to the Bastille, and lodged as well as he could be
in that castle. He was refused nothing that he desired.
His greatest liking was for linen of an extraordinary
fineness and for lace; he played on the guitar. He had the
very best of everything, and the Governor rarely sat
down in his presence. An old physician of the Bastille,
who had often attended this strange gentleman in his
illnesses, stated that he never saw his face, though he
had frequently examined his tongue and other parts of
his body. He was admirably made, said this doctor; his
skin was rather brown; the very tone of his voice was
interesting, never complaining of his situation, and never
disclosing who he was.

This stranger died in 1704, and was buried at night in
the parish of St Paul. What redoubles our astonishment
is that, when he was sent to the Isle of Sainte-Marguerite,
no person of any consequence disappeared in Europe.
This prisoner was such a one without doubt, however,
for this is what happened in his first days after arriving
on the island; the Governor himself used to set the silver
plates upon his table and then retire, having locked the
door. One day the prisoner wrote with a knife upon a
silver plate, and threw the plate out of the window
towards a boat which was on the river, near the foot of
the tower. A fisherman to whom the boat belonged
picked up the plate and brought it to the Governor. He,
astonished, asked the fisherman: 'Have you read what is

written upon this plate, or has anyone seen it in your possession?' 'I do not know how to read,' replied the fisherman, 'I have just found it, and nobody has seen it.' The peasant was detained till the Governor was convinced that he could not read, and that the plate had been seen by no other person. 'Go,' said he, 'you are lucky in not knowing how to read.' There are some very credible witnesses of this fact, who are now living.

There is another version of this story in which the fisherman has changed profession. A Catholic priest, Father Papon, writing about the masked man in his *History of Provence*, tells the story of a barber and a shirt:

I found in the citadel an Officer of the Free Company, who was seventy-nine years old. He told me several times that a barber of that company had noticed one day, under the prisoner's window, something white floating on the water; he went to pick it up and took it to Monsieur de St Mars. It was a very fine shirt, screwed up into a ball, which the prisoner had written all over. Monsieur de St Mars, having unfolded it and read a few lines, asked the barber with an air of embarrassment, if he had not had the curiosity to read what he had found. The barber protested several times that he had read nothing; but, two days afterwards, he was found dead in his bed.

By 1771 Voltaire had turned these rumours into a theory. He had become convinced that the man in the mask was in fact an illegitimate son of Queen Anne and Cardinal Mazarin, then Richelieu's deputy. In a publisher's note inserted into his second edition of 1771, he explained:

The Iron Mask was without doubt a brother, and an elder brother, of Louis xiv, whose mother had that taste for fine linen [as the masked man supposedly had] . . . reading the contemporary memoirs in which this anecdote of the Queen finds mention, which gave me the same taste of the man in the Iron Mask, I had not a doubt that this was her son, a conclusion which all the other circumstances had already convinced me of. It is known that Louis XIII had long ceased to live with the Queen; that the birth of Louis XIV was merely the fruit of a 'happy accident' skilfully brought about, a 'chance' which absolutely obliged the King to sleep in the same bed as the Queen. Here, then, is how I believe the event came about: the Queen had come to persuade herself that it was her fault that no heir had been born to Louis XIII. The birth of the Iron Mask undeceived her on that point. The Cardinal [Richelieu] to whom she had confessed her secret, saw where his advantage lay in it. He imagined shaping it at once to his own profit and to the profit of the state. Satisfied, by this example, that the Queen was able to give children to the King, as a consequence of this proof, the accident of there being only one bed for the King and Queen was arranged. But both Queen and Cardinal being equally persuaded of the necessity of concealing from Louis XIII the existence of the Iron Mask, they had the child removed in secret. The secret was kept from Louis XIV until after the death of Cardinal Mazarin. But the King, discovering that he had a brother living, an elder brother, moreover, whom his mother could not possibly disown, and in whom some signal likeness might not improbably declare his origin, and reflecting that this child, born in wedlock, could not, without the gravest consequences and most dire scandal, be pronounced illegitimate after the decease of Louis XIII, Louis XIV could have fallen on no measure wiser or more just than the one which he had adopted to secure his own safety; and that measure, in addition, while securing his own safety and the tranquillity of the state, at the same time spared him an act of cruelty which a soveriegn less conscientious and less magnanimous would have accepted as necessary.

At this point Voltaire also revised the date of the masked man's death, from 1704 to the 3rd March, 1703.

Voltaire's theory was a less fantastic version than
Dumas', of the common idea that the man in the mask was
an unwanted brother or half-brother of the king. It is
important to examine every such rumour and every theory;
and the popularity of the 'two brothers' idea over the years
is such that it must be seriously considered in the final
reckoning. But Voltaire's version too is full of inconsistencies and inaccuracies that do not tally with the known facts.
Quite apart from the inadequacies of supporting a claim
for blood ties upon a mutual liking for linen, the solution
simply cannot be as straightforward as Voltaire seems to
think. We know that the prisoner was not thrown into gaol
until 1666 at the earliest, when St Mars and Louvois had
both been installed in their respective posts. But if he was
indeed a son of Louis XIII, a twin or elder brother to Louis
XIV, he would have been born no later than 1638, making
him not less than 28 – hardly the easily manipulated child
of legend, but a full grown member of society for many
years before his arrest. Even if he was an illegitimate son of
the queen, but conceived after the birth of Louis XIV, and
before Louis XIII's death in 1643, he could still have been
no younger than 23. But Voltaire claims that he was
imprisoned upon the death of Cardinal Mazarin in 1661,
which is at least five years too early to fit these facts.

Furthermore, an illegitimate birth would have been
impossible for the queen to conceal from all the courtiers
and her many attendants. Even if she had managed it, the
child would probably have been discreetly given another
identity, rather than imprisoned in such incredible conditions. History is peppered with the illegitimate sons of
royalty: they were usually given titles and large incomes.
Louis XIV himself had ten accredited bastards. We are
searching for someone much more out of the ordinary –
someone so unusual that the authorities would be *likely* to
punish him in this way.

Of course, Voltaire's dates proved to be wrong as well,
as the records show. St Mars took over the Bastille in 1698,
not in 1690, and the masked man died on 19 November

1703, not on the 3rd March of that year, or indeed in 1704. Louvois did not pay a visit to the prisoner at Sainte-Marguerite but at Pignerol (where he was first imprisoned) in the year 1670, as will become clear.

For all its inaccuracies, the theory was given a great deal of credibility at the time. One variant even suggests that the masked man was an illegitimate son of the king and one Madame Lafayette, which would be even less remarkable and would make the whole extraordinary affair quite pointless. Yet the authorities were sufficiently worried about the spread of such ideas that in 1746 they banned a romance entitled *The Iron Mask, or the Admirable Adventures of a Father and Son*, concerning two secret lovers who are arrested, encased in masks of iron and sent to an island prison. It is unlikely that the author, the Chevalier du Mouhy, had any satirical intent – more likely he had simply overheard an intriguing story – but it shows that as the story became more well known, the government became more desperate to stamp it out. Louis xiv had been more cunning. While he was still alive, false rumours and stories had been actually planted rather than deterred, to confuse interested parties; and it was almost certainly one of these that Voltaire fell for, in producing his rather lame theory. For it is now established that Voltaire based it primarily on the evidence of the mistress of the minister of war at the time – the very minister responsible for spreading such stories and guarding the secret.

Now that a clear picture has been drawn of what was generally presumed at the time, and of what is known for sure today, the next step must be to question the witnesses; to examine every description of the man in the mask, by anyone who caught a glimpse of him, in order to put together the most comprehensive picture possible of this elusive subject.

Notes on Chapter 4

1 Cardinal Mazarin, chief minister of France, who succeeded Cardinal Richelieu.

5

The men who saw the mask

In a sense, we are about to hear the testimony of the witnesses for the defence. For their accounts are often at variance with the official or semi-official explanations. As the prosecution might readily point out, they are an easy group of witnesses to discredit: some with criminal records, some writing years later about a fleeting glimpse down a corridor. But what is essential to bear in mind is that these eyewitnesses have absolutely no reason to obscure the truth, unlike their official counterparts. Why should they distort a small part of a large mystery that they would never understand? For us, they are vital in determining the age and past circumstances of the mysterious prisoner.

Our first witness is, on paper, perhaps the least trustworthy of all. Constantin de Renneville was a double agent, a French spy who had been caught red-handed, spying traitorously against his own country, and had been sentenced to several years in the Bastille as a result. De Renneville considered himself to be a political prisoner, and upon his release in 1715 wrote a book 'exposing' the regime that had punished him. He said that he thought it was 1704 when he saw the masked man, a date which we know to be incorrect; but having spent so many years in prison, and having probably lost track of time, it would not be surprising if he had got his dates mixed up. He wrote:

I saw a prisoner ... whose name I was never able to learn: But Ru, the turnkey, leading me back into my chamber, told me that he had been a prisoner for thirty-one years; that M. de St Mars had brought him with him from the Isle of Sainte-Marguerite ... I saw him in a room into which I was introduced by accident. Seeing me come in, the officers made him turn his back towards me, which prevented me from seeing his face. He was a man of medium height, well built with very thick, dense black hair, which he wore in a pony-tail, of which not one had gone grey.

When pressed, the turnkey told de Renneville only that he was a religious prisoner. As we know, St Mars only brought one prisoner from the Isle of Sainte-Marguerite to the Bastille, the prisoner he had guarded since his days at Pignerol, so this must be our man. He was at the Bastille from 1698 to 1703, so – going back thirty-one years – this means that he must have been arrested between 1667 and 1672, which tallies with everything else that we know so far. Only catching sight of the back of his head, de Renneville said that the man's hair seemed to be thick and black, an uncommon colour; but absolutely every other eyewitness who mentioned his hair said that it was white. Certainly, at that age, after so many years in a cell, it should have been white. What seems to have happened is that de Renneville had glimpsed the back of his black velvet mask. The pony-tail, presumably, was part of the fastening.

Staying within the Bastille, we now have a medical testimony. A number of doctors treated the masked man, but only one dared to put his recollections down on paper. This was a junior doctor named Marsolan, who with his father-in-law Doctor Fresquier often treated the masked man. Of course, he never saw his face, which stayed masked, but he examined his body and was allowed to talk to him about purely medical matters. Doctor Marsolan's testimony has already been picked up by Voltaire: 'He was admirably made, said this Doctor; his skin was rather brown; the very tone of his voice was interesting, never complaining of his situation, and never disclosing who he was.'

From their brief conversations the doctor gleaned one vital piece of evidence; the masked man himself said that he was about 60 years old, although he did not remember his exact age. This means that we are looking for a man born in either the late 1630s or early 1640s, which neither confirms nor rules out a connection with Louis XIV, but does confirm that he was about 30 years old at the time of his arrest. If he had been examined on arrival that would put his date of birth at about 1638. We can forget any thoughts of an unwanted child; whatever the masked man had said or done, he had waited thirty years to do it.

There is one other medical reference which must be mentioned, although it probably has no bearing on our investigation. According to one French author, a Doctor Nelaton once treated an Englishman in the Bastille, whose face was covered with a towel. He was not masked, but the very fact that he had a towel over his head suggests that his presence there was not intended to be common knowledge. Perhaps this could have been our man, although other witnesses stated that the masked man was French, and no others at all remark upon his being English; it is worth bearing in mind, however, because there are theories that have yet to be examined, which maintain that the masked man was an Englishman, or someone with an English connection.

Two other prisoners managed to communicate briefly with the masked man. One, the Abbot Lenglet, only had time to discover that he was 'much travelled'. But another prisoner managed a whole conversation, whispered down a communicating chimney. His name is Dubuisson, and he was incarcerated on the fourth floor of the Bertaudière Tower in the Bastille, which means that at some point our prisoner was put in a cell on the third floor. Dubuisson attempted to prise the secret of his incarceration from the masked man, but he would not reveal either his name or his crime. He explained that if he were to tell Dubuisson anything, they would both be put to death instantly.

A number of investigators have tried to concoct theories from the disposition of the rooms in the Bertaudière Tower, but it is a thankless task. For unlike the other towers in the Bastille, which each had one cell per floor, de Renneville tells us that the Bertaudière Tower had four rooms on each floor. De Renneville lived on the second floor, but only managed to communicate with one prisoner on the floor above, who was an Italian Abbot. As we shall see, this in turn has spawned various theories that the masked man was an Italian clergyman, although there is nothing definite to connect the prisoner above de Renneville with the prisoner below Dubuisson. We also know that a witch named Anne Randon was imprisoned on the third floor in 1701, but no-one has seriously claimed that we should be looking for the woman in the iron mask.[1]

The masked man came to be known in gaol as the 'ancient prisoner' – a term used in all official correspondence and by du Jonca, the king's lieutenant who has already been of such help to us. At one stage du Jonca entered a confusing reference in his journal, that he had put two prisoners – one a political offender, one sexual – 'in the second room of the Bertaudière Tower, with the ancient prisoner, both being well locked in.' This has been taken to mean that all three were crammed in together; yet another variation. But at this stage the ancient prisoner was still in the 'third single room' of the tower, so surely du Jonca meant only that they were on the same floor; at four rooms to a floor, the 'third room' would have been on the ground floor. In the light of what we know about the severity of his imprisonment, it is highly unlikely that he would have shared a room to save space! It is difficult to avoid the conclusion that too many investigators have been led astray by technicalities such as these.

More fundamental is the evidence of our next witness, a man named William Louis de Formanoir. De Formanoir was related to St Mars, and his father was one of St Mars' lieutenants, as was his great-uncle's cousin Blainvilliers. Blainvilliers revealed all he knew to his young relative. The younger de Formanoir relates:

I am going to tell you what I know of this prisoner. He was only known in the Isles of Sainte-Marguerite and at the Bastille under the name of 'La Tour' [The Tower]. The governor and the other officers showed great deference to him; he obtained everything that could be granted to a prisoner. He often went for walks, always with a mask on his face. It is only since *The Century of Louis XIV* by Voltaire was published that I have heard it said that the mask was of iron and with springs; perhaps this detail was forgotten when I was told about the matter; but he only wore the mask when he went out to take the air, or when he was obliged to talk to some stranger. Monsieur de Blainvilliers, an infantry officer who had access to Monsieur de St Mars, the governor of the Isle of Sainte-Marguerite and later of the Bastille, told me several times that as the fate of 'La Tour' had greatly excited his curiosity, to satisfy it he took the clothes and the weapons of a soldier who was to be on sentry duty in a gallery under the window of the room which this prisoner occupied at the Isles of Sainte-Marguerite; that from there he had seen him very well; that he was not wearing his mask, that his face was white, his body large and well-built, his calves were a little too well developed and his hair was white although he was only in the prime of life. He had spent almost that entire night walking about his room. Blainvilliers added that he was always clothed in brown, that he was given good linen and books; that the governor and the officers remained standing and bare-headed before him until he told them to put their hats on and be seated; that they often went to keep him company and eat with him . . . Monsieur de Blainvilliers told me that when he died in 1704 he was buried secretly in St Paul and that chemicals were put in the coffin to eat the body away. I have never heard anybody say that he had a foreign accent.

This is very important. With the exception of the reference to his dying in 1704, which is probably taken from Voltaire, it fits all the known facts and is of great value to us. Except – there was no gallery under the prisoner's window at Sainte-Marguerite, only the cliffs and the open sea. At first sight this seems to put de Formanoir's story into question; but in fact he had probably just got his locations muddled. There was almost certainly a gallery under the masked man's window at Pignerol – St Mars had been specifically instructed that his window should not open directly on to the courtyard like all the others, hence the private gallery. And the gaoler Blainvilliers was transferred to Metz in 1681, long before St Mars and the masked man ever reached Sainte-Marguerite. Far more likely that he would have tried to snatch a look at a new prisoner when he first arrived, than wait another two or three decades. And at Pignerol the prisoner would indeed have been 'in the prime of life', whereas he would have been well into middle age by the time he was incarcerated in his island prison. Assuming that Blainvilliers did indeed see the masked man at Pignerol, the story does confirm that we are looking for a white-haired Frenchman, and it gives him another name – 'La Tour', or, 'The Tower'. So when we come to investigate any official archives, we are now looking out for any references to a 'La Tour' or to an 'ancient prisoner'. And one more odd thing, which may only be an exaggeration – Blainvilliers said that the Governor and his officials removed their hats in the prisoner's presence: a courtesy usually reserved for those with royal connections.

De Formanoir also relates the story of the journey from Sainte-Marguerite to the Bastille, on which the masked man was accompanied by St Mars, Major Rosarges, Blainvilliers, Chaplain Giraut, the turnkey Antoine Ru and a driver called Lecurjer, who later became captain of the gates at the Bastille. The party made an overnight stop at de Formanoir's home, the Château of Palteau[2], which then belonged to St Mars. It was a visit which stirred the imagination of the local peasants. As a young man, de Formanoir heard their reminiscences personally:

> In 1698, Monsieur de St Mars moved on from the governorship of the Isles of Sainte-Marguerite to that of the Bastille. While coming to take possession, he broke journey with his prisoner at his estate of Palteau. The masked man arrived in a litter which preceded that of Monsieur de St Mars; they were accompanied by several men on horseback. The peasants went before their Lord. Monsieur de St Mars ate with his prisoner, whose back was turned to the casement windows of the dining room which gave on to the courtyard. The peasants that I questioned could not see whether he ate with his mask on, but they saw very clearly that St Mars, who sat opposite him, had two pistols by him at the table. They were served by only one valet [Antoine Ru], who fetched the dishes brought to him in the antechamber, carefully closing the door of the dining room behind him. When the prisoner crossed the courtyard he always had his black mask on his face; the peasants noticed that his teeth and his lips could be seen; that he was tall and had white hair. Monsieur de St Mars slept in a bed that had been made up beside that of the masked man.

The Château of Palteau still exists, and the room where the masked man dined – now a kitchen – can still be seen. Even a century later, the memory of the distinguished, white-haired old prisoner lingered on amongst the peasants of Palteau. There is, perhaps, one other point worth mentioning. De Formanoir speaks of the arrival of two litters at Palteau; Du Jonca recorded their arrival at the Bastille together in one litter. It was a simple attempt at a security measure: two litters would show that there were two very important people arriving, and St Mars didn't want that known.

We have been assisted in the collection of eyewitness accounts by Father Papon, the local Provençal historian who recorded the tale of the barber and the shirt. He visited the island of Sainte-Marguerite soon after the events he described took place, and he was shown the room where the ancient prisoner had lived. The walls were very thick, and there was only one north-facing window, looking down to the sea and to the rocks below, which was blocked off by multiple iron grilles. Two sentries had stood facing the sea on the rocks below the masked man's room, with orders to shoot at any boat that came near.

Clearly, the security precautions surrounding this man were staggering. Two stories related by Father Papon seem to confirm this. The first tells how St Mars was visited by the son of a friend, who was wandering around the prison when he saw his host standing in the doorway of the masked man's cell. The young man was curious to hear what was being said and walked up the corridor; but St Mars saw him coming, slammed the door shut and hurried him away. The young man was immediately questioned to find out whether he had heard anything, and when St Mars was absolutely satisfied that he had not, he was packed off the same day. St Mars wrote to his friend, saying that the episode had nearly cost his son dear, and that he was sending him home in case anything similar happened.

The second story tells how a woman from a nearby village heard that St Mars was looking for a servant for a very important prisoner whose valet had just died. Hoping to make her fortune, she applied for the job, only to discover that she was to serve the masked prisoner, and that she would be expected to live under the same conditions. She would be locked away, forbidden to speak or leave the prison, forbidden to see her children or her family ever again, a life of well-guarded monotony relieved only by the brief occasions when she would be brought in to serve her faceless master. It is not surprising that she turned the job down, nor is it surprising that St Mars never found anybody from outside to fill the position.

The islands of Sainte-Marguerite yield one more important witness, a playwright named Lagrange-Chancel, who

was a prisoner there soon after the masked man's departure, and who later escaped by hijacking a fishing boat and
making for Sardinia. Not long after the death of Louis xiv,
he badgered the new governor, Lamotte-Guérin, to tell him
about the 'ancient prisoner'. Lamotte-Guérin had been the
king's lieutenant at Sainte-Marguerite, in the same position
as du Jonca at the Bastille, and the Cannes parish register
shows us that he had been there since 1693 – so, like du
Jonca he would seem to be a reliable witness, in an official
position, without being privy to the conspiracy. The
governor informed the playwright categorically that the
masked prisoner had first been gaoled in 1669, which was
written in the prison register. He also recounted a brief
exchange between the prisoner and St Mars: the masked
man had asked,

'Does the King want my life?'

Whereupon St Mars had replied,

'No my Prince, your life is safe, you have only to allow
yourself to be led.'

This is crucial because – apart from suggesting that the
gaolers thought they had a prince on their hands – it firmly
identifies 1669 as a definite date for the arrest of the masked
man, a date which tallies with what we already know. So
we are looking for someone about 30 years old, who
disappeared in 1669.

Lamotte-Guérin thought that perhaps the Duke of Beaufort had been the mysterious prisoner; whoever it was, he
said,

St Mars had a great respect for this prisoner, that he
always served him himself, on silver plates, and often
furnished him with clothing as richly as he could desire.

The author St Foix bears this out, researching the story in
the light of Voltaire's book:

It is certain that Madame Le Bret, mother of the late Monsieur Le Bret, First President and Steward of Provence, used to choose in Paris, at the request of Monsieur de St Mars, her close friend, the finest linen and the best lace, and send them to him, at the Isle of Sainte-Marguerite, for this prisoner, which confirms what Monsieur Voltaire has reported.

But apart from this apparent taste for luxury, the prisoner was a quiet man, explained Lamotte-Guérin. He would spend the lonely hours with a little pair of tweezers, plucking hairs from the beard that he had grown.

There is one more witness, who has left us with more of a puzzle than a statement. This is Chamillart, the last royal minister to know the secret and to look after the affairs of the masked man. It is true that he is an 'official' source, and so does not really belong among these witnesses, but unlike his colleagues Chamillart was not so ready with a tall tale when questioned; in fact he never told anybody anything. That is, until he lay close to death at the age of 70 in 1721, when his son-in-law got down on bended knees and begged him to reveal the secret. Chamillart replied that it was a state secret and that he had taken an oath never to betray it. But as he was dying, he left his son with a cryptic reference to puzzle over; that the masked prisoner was 'a man who knew all the secrets of Monsieur Fouquet'.

Voltaire drew rather too much from this. He wrote:

> Now, why such unheard of precautions for a confidante of M. Fouquet, for a subaltern? The belief is, that during this period, nobody of any consequence disappeared. Thus it is clear that this was a prisoner of the greatest importance, whose destiny had always been a secret. This is all that we can allow ourselves to surmise.

Not necessarily. For both Fouquet and his masked confidant were imprisoned in the same gaol – Pignerol, the king's alpine fortress. Could it be that they knew each other, that they had conversed there? Fouquet had been the most important minister in France before his fall. And the masked man's secret, as a piece of information that threatened the security of the state, would have been no secret to him. Perhaps he too, in his time, was party to the great plan to bury the secret once and for all.

Notes on Chapter 5

1 One Maître Bouche tried this line, but it has long since been given up as a very silly idea.
2 Situated between Joigny and Villeneuve-le-Roi. Ownership of the château formally passed down the de Formanoir branch of the family when St Mars died.

6

A royal deception

Of those who devised or carried out the plot to imprison
the masked man, Chamillart was the last to die and the
only one to leave a clue behind intentionally – that the
masked prisoner had some connection with Fouquet, and
perhaps knew him. His two predecessors as ministers
responsible for the prisoner, Louvois and Barbezieux[1], had
died in 1691 and 1701 respectively, very possibly murdered
by the king's agents. Louis xiv himself had died in 1715;
his gaoler St Mars had outlived the masked man by only
five years, dying in 1708, preceded by Etienne du Jonca in
1706, Major Rosarges in 1707, and followed by Antoine Ru
in 1713.

But the secret had not died with Chamillart. Perhaps
because Chamillart still lived, or perhaps gripped with
guilt, the king felt that he had to let his successor into the
secret before he died. So it was that he told everything to
his nephew the Duke of Orléans, who became prince regent
for the new king – Louis xv, Louis xiv's five-year-old great-
grandson. Philippe of Orléans was to tell the boy the truth
when he came of age. Of course the young king could
hardly wait to discover the secret, and pressed the duke to
reveal it, but the impassive Orléans refused to say anything
until the day named by the old king. When the day finally
arrived, Orléans drew him aside in front of all the lords of
court and whispered the secret of the man in the mask. It
must have had a profound effect. The king stood silent

except to say: 'If he were still alive today I would give him his freedom.'

Of course everybody now pressed Louis xv to reveal the truth, but he would not. All he would admit to his daughter was that:

'Nobody has ever yet said the truth about the iron mask.'

To the Duke of Choiseul he said:

'All conjectures which have been made hitherto on this subject are false.'

Even his valet asked him about it, but Louis would only say:

'You would like me to tell you something on this subject. Well, you will know something more than others. That is that the imprisonment of this unfortunate person harmed no-one but himself.'

Louis xv was certainly interested in the subject – he kept a copy of a banned book about it on his library shelves at Choisy.[2] But the Baroness de Gleichen, who knew him well, wrote that he never revealed the secret to anybody. Questioned by his family, he explained that he was bound by an oath not to tell. But one important fact has come of his apparent refusal to divulge anything: that we are not to believe any theory formulated before the 1720s. This at least rules out many of the conjectures already spread by the king's own predecessor.

Louis xv did not feel bound by the same sense of duty – or perhaps guilt – as his great-grandfather. When his son begged him to pass on the secret in turn, Louis xv refused, saying, 'It is good that you should not know it. It would cause you too much pain.'

And it is here that direct knowledge of the secret finally ended. Louis xvi, later beheaded in the French Revolution, made a frantic search to discover who the masked man really was. Egged on by his wife Marie Antoinette, he ordered Maurepas to search through the massive volumes of state papers in search of clues; but Maurepas found very little. Eventually he concluded that the mysterious prisoner was in fact an Italian diplomat, a theory that is now accepted by most historians as the correct one, despite much contradictory and confusing evidence. Madame de Campan, a friend of the royal couple, wrote at the time:

> I was with the Queen when the King, having finished his researches, told her that he had found nothing in the secret papers relevant to the existence of this prisoner; that he had spoken on the subject with Monsieur de Maurepas, whose age brought him nearer the time when this story must have been known to the Minister, and that Monsieur de Maurepas had assured him that here was a prisoner of a very dangerous character through his intriguing spirit, and a subject of the Duke of Mantua.

The king accused Maurepas of lying, a charge that Maurepas strenuously denied. In fact there was an Italian diplomat called Mattioli imprisoned in Pignerol during the period in question, but it now seems likely that his name was deliberately spread at the time to throw people off the scent.

But more of Mattioli later. For the present, it is clear that we are dealing with a royal secret, both personal and political, and that King Louis xiv would stop at nothing – short of killing his prisoner – to prevent it leaking out. At the time, nobody dared speak about the matter, except in private. The diarist St Simon tells us that all the court mail passed through the hands of censors. The letters sent by the gaoler St Mars to Paris about his charge seem to have nearly all been destroyed and no record kept of their ever having been received. So it is vitally important to bear in mind that there was a thorough cover-up in operation, now that we come to hear the evidence – as it were – 'for the prosecution': that is to say, the evidence of those in authority or their friends, who sought to dismiss the masked man, to connect him with obscure and unimportant crimes, or to reduce him to the status of just another embarrassing illegitimate child. Not only is their testimony automatically discredited by the very fact that they are giving evidence, against all orders and against all precedent, where others were too terrified to do so; but it is also worth noting just how contradictory all the stories are. Hardly any of the testimonies you are about to read agree with each other, in contrast to the evidence of the accidental or unbiased witnesses of the previous chapter. In fact, to stretch a point, it is possible to say that each of these semi-official theories can be discounted from the investigation. They may lead us close to the real answer, for all the best deceptions are close enough to the truth to sound realistic, but the very fact that these stories were being offered at all should be grounds enough to distrust them. In retrospect, Louis xv certainly did not think them worth listening to.

The most common theories allowed to circulate through the court unchecked at the time were those naming the masked man as an unwanted royal child. We have already seen one: Abbot Soulavie's story of the twin king born in the evening, which was picked up by Dumas for his 'Three Musketeers' adventure. This is supposed to have come from Prince Regent Orléans, who told Mademoiselle Valois everything in return for sleeping with him. Yet is it really likely that a man so conscientious as to keep his mouth shut for a decade on the instructions of a dead king, who supposedly never revealed the secret to a soul, would spill everything to a casual sexual partner? Far more likely that he would invent a plausible story that would affect nobody living, in order to fend off a persistently curious lady and to manipulate her at the same time.

Other variations on this story are manifold – that the masked man was a son of Louis xiv and his cousin Henrietta of Orléans (but they already had a son – the Marquis de Verdes), or a son of the Count de Guiche and the Queen of Sweden, or even the daughter of Queen Anne by a (no doubt large and potent) black slave. The French author P. M. Dijol decided in 1978 that the masked man was not only black, but a dwarf and the secret lover of

Louis xiv's queen: nicknamed 'Ali' because of his blackness
and 'Marquis' because of the royal connection, this
accounted for the grave-name 'Marchioly'. Monsieur
Dijol's theory may be nonsensical rubbish, but at least it is
ingenious enough to include a reason for masking the
prisoner. Unfortunately we know that he was at liberty for
some thirty years before being arrested and hidden away.
The Baron de Gleichen, by contrast, confidently attributed
the 'masked man' to the queen and Cardinal Mazarin, a
story later picked up by Voltaire.

The next semi-official witness has a similar story, that
confirms the existence of a deliberate campaign to circulate
realistic-sounding nonsense. She is Madame St Quentin,
the mistress of Barbezieux, the minister of war, who was
responsible for the masked man for ten years. In fact
Barbezieux was the son of the Marquis de Louvois; he
inherited the post when his father was mysteriously
poisoned in 1691, and it passed on to Chamillart when
Barbezieux died in turn in 1701. Madame St Quentin,
pressed by her friends, urged Barbezieux to reveal the
secret of the masked man. He told her that the prisoner
was actually the son of Queen Anne and the Duke of
Buckingham, conceived on Buckingham's state visit to
France in 1626 and imprisoned upon the death of her
protector Cardinal Mazarin in 1661.

It is certainly true that the Duke of Buckingham made a
state visit from England to France in 1626, and was
involved in a public flirtation with the queen, which makes
the story sound plausible. In fact, Buckingham – a high-
handed, arrogant, spendthrift nincompoop – arrived in
Paris with 700 retainers and a series of costumes covered in
pearls and diamonds, which had been deliberately sewn on
loosely in order to fall off in public. The queen seemed
flattered by these ludicrous antics, and by the lavish praise
that he bestowed upon her, but they never went far from
the public gaze together. On the one occasion that Buckingham did attempt to have his way with her, in the garden

at Amiens, she screamed for help; and the duke's improper advances were rewarded by a hefty thumping from Putange, her equerry. It is almost impossible that the pair conceived a child, let alone that Anne gave birth to one later without anybody noticing. Quite apart from that, we know that 1661 is too early a date for the masked man's arrest, and that he was some years short of his late seventies by the time of his death. The same question must also be applied to all such stories – why bother to mask such a child?

Another man to spread misleading rumours was St Mars, allegedly the Prince Regent's source for the story of the unwanted twin. A reference in a surviving letter which St Mars wrote to Louvois in 1670 discredits this and the other stories that have been accredited to him. He wrote:

> There are people who are sometimes so curious in asking me for information about my prisoner, or the reason I take so many precautions for his security, that I am obliged to tell them tall stories.

St Mars told local people on the Isle of Sainte-Marguerite that the masked man was the son of the English dictator Oliver Cromwell or the Emperor of China, or the 'Grand Turk'. But the most popular story in the neighbourhood was that the masked man was in fact François de Vendôme, Duke of Beaufort, the High Admiral of France who had disappeared at the siege of Candia on 25 June 1669.

Candia is now the Port of Heraklion in Crete. At the time it was a fortress held by 6000 desperate Venetians against a massive horde of fanatical Turks at the gates. Beaufort, an illegitimate cousin of the king and a trusted friend of the royal family, a man who had been as an uncle to the young Louis, was charged to go to its aid. Renowned for his boldness and bravery, he was the obvious man for the job. Weighing anchor on 5 June, it took only two weeks under sail to reach Crete; and on the night of the 25th, Beaufort's ships slipped into Candia harbour with a force of soldiers on board ready to do battle.

The French attack succeeded brilliantly. Led by Beaufort

himself, they put the Turks to flight, and were in hot
pursuit when a spark ignited a 25-ton Turkish powder
magazine; the massive explosion destroyed an entire French
company. As the terrified and panic-stricken troops ran
this way and that, not knowing what had attacked them,
Beaufort tried to rally his men in the darkness and confusion. As the Turks regrouped he plunged into the smoke
shouting, 'To me my children! I am your Admiral! Rally
around me!' – and was never seen again.

Although there is no concrete evidence to prove it,
Beaufort's candidature was probably spread by St Mars as
well; certainly, by the time of the governor Lamotte-Guérin
– whose views we have already encountered – it had become
accepted as the official story on Sainte-Marguerite. Sup-
porters of the Beaufort theory do have one other card to
play: the curious contention that 'Marchiali' – a version of
the name on the masked man's grave – is an anagram of
'Hic Amiral', French/Latin for 'here is the Admiral'. That
may be so, but the name on the death certificate was
actually spelt 'Marchioly', and anyway, why anybody
trying to hide a corpse should start putting up Latin puzzles
on headstones is beyond understanding. Neither does the
Beaufort theory provide any explanation at all as to why
anyone should go to the trouble of abducting a perfectly
ordinary courtier and soldier from the middle of a battle,
imprisoning him and masking him; but it is interesting that
the authorities wished to push the story. For the duke
disappeared in 1669 and, as we know from the Sainte-
Marguerite prison register, that was when the masked man
was first incarcerated. This only goes to confirm the
accuracy of the 1669 figure, for it shows that they were
looking for a fake candidate who filled the date. But the
poor Duke of Beaufort, who probably lay dead in the soil
outside Candia, was born in 1616; and would have been
almost 90 when the masked man died in 1703.

Perhaps the most realistic story concerns Mattioli, the
Italian diplomat, who is accepted by most historians as the
masked man. We have seen how King Louis xvi, deprived

of the secret by Louis xv, could find only Mattioli as a realistic candidate. Another royal mistress was the one to originate this story: Madame de Pompadour, the mistress of Louis xv, was told by her lover that the masked prisoner was the minister of an Italian Prince, which is a clear reference to Mattioli. It is hardly likely that King Louis xv – who never told a soul, not even his own son – would reveal the real secret to a talkative mistress; or that he would describe the purely political imprisonment of the Italian diplomat as 'too painful' to pass on to his offspring, some seventy years after the event. But it is very likely that he would use the obviously tried and trusted method of spreading false rumours through an indiscreet mistress to throw later investigators off the scent.

Another damning factor against the Mattioli theory is the masked man's death certificate, reproduced in chapter 2. At first sight it appears to be a reasonably substantial document, but in fact it contains only one accurate piece of information – the date of death. The rest, such as the age 'forty-five', was manufactured for public consumption. This includes the name, 'Marchioly' or 'Martioly' which sounds uncommonly like 'Mattioli'. Why was that particular name chosen as an alias out of a million possibilities, if not deliberately to lead people into making the same connection? It was certainly not chosen to divert attention from an Italian called Mattioli. This burial name seems to have been relatively common currency in the Bastille in some form or another, which is suspicious considering how little else was revealed about him: for instance, the turnkey Antoine Ru told the inquisitive Constantin de Renneville that the masked man had been imprisoned as a boy for instigating anti-Jesuit propaganda, which is probably the worst story yet.

Our last witness is Madame Palatine, the sister-in-law of King Louis xiv himself. That she was not part of the plot is obvious; while Louis was still alive, she dared to write to her friend the Electress Sophia of Hanover, about a rumour she had heard:

A man remained long years in the Bastille, and has died there, masked. He had at his side two musketeers ready to kill him if he took off his mask. He ate and slept masked. It must have undoubtedly been so because in other respects he was well treated, well lodged, and was given all that he wished for. He went to communion masked: he was very devout and read continually. No-one has ever been able to learn who he was.

Madame Palatine decided to make enquiries and perhaps even asked the king himself. At any rate the authorities satisfied her. Twelve days later she wrote another letter:

I have just learnt who the masked man was, who died in the Bastille. His wearing the mask was not due to cruelty. He was an English Lord who had been mixed up in the affair of the Duke of Berwick against King William. He died there so that the King might never learn what became of him.

The Duke of Berwick was the son of King James II of England, who had been deposed by King William III in 1689. Berwick had tried to unseat the new King. This is one of a few references to a masked Englishman, but like the others it contains limp reasoning and very little substance: by 1689 the ancient prisoner had been languishing in his cell for twenty years.

The most common theory of this kind is that the masked man was really the Duke of Monmouth, the beloved son of Charles II and his mistress Lucy Waters. When Charles died, his unpopular Catholic brother James II had ascended the English throne, and Monmouth – although he had no real claim to replace him – felt that his hour had come. It hadn't. Monmouth was roundly defeated by James at the Battle of Sedgemoor in 1683, and met his death soon after on the scaffold. The very nature of his execution rather precludes any idea that he was still alive in 1703. James was not the sort of man to show mercy, and despite all Monmouth's whimpering entreaties and beseechings, he found himself facing the axe on a July morning in front of a huge, appalled crowd who were with him to a man. Perhaps it was the visible terror of the executioner at the ugly mood of the spectators that allowed the Duke to compose himself; calm at the last, he didn't let them down. The unhappy executioner was not so lucky. He took five nervous blows to sever the head, the first one so poor that Monmouth raised his head from the block with a look of reproach. As the fifth and final blow fell, the tension in the crowd was released, and they rushed foward to lynch the executioner and dip their fingers in the duke's hallowed blood.

The manner of his death and the rather large number of furious spectators somewhat spoils the idea that he was the masked man – for Monmouth spent the first half of the ancient prisoner's captivity at liberty and was most certainly dead during the second half. And of course, there could be no conceivable reason for masking the Duke of Monmouth, the Duke of Berwick, or any other known Englishman.

So if we are to believe the stories originated by Louis xiv, Louis xv and their ministers, and spread by their mistresses and servants, the masked man was in fact two English noblemen, a naughty schoolboy, a French duke, an Italian diplomat, the emperor of China, a Turkish sultan, the son of Oliver Cromwell and the offspring of at least five affairs, making him part French, part English, part Swedish, part Italian, part Turkish, part Chinese, and very possibly black.

Once Louis xv had died, the identity of the masked man was anybody's guess, but because there was nobody who knew the real answer to tell lies about it, guessing became a more sensible game. The attitude of the authorities changed: unlike Louis xiv, who was happy to let gossips call the morals of his family and his government into question if it obscured the truth, later governments were less happy to have Bourbon morality questioned, but were equally keen to get to the bottom of the mystery. But the ingenuity of their predecessors was to thwart them, leaving them with only a tangle of inaccurate stories and half-truths: to this day nobody has found a workable answer, because nobody has set out all the facts and proceeded to work out an answer that fitted each and every one. One thing that we can be sure of is that all the 'official' theories are red herrings, with the possible exception of the Mattioli theory, where there will be a much stronger case to answer. So now that some of the historical red tape has been disentangled it is time to look at the evidence so far and assemble a few conclusions.

Notes on Chapter 6

1 A third minister, Ponchartrain, was partially responsible for a very brief spell during the period 1698–99.
2 *The History of Persia*, so named because to write scurrilous books about France it was necessary to pretend that you were writing about another country.

7

Speculation

We now know enough to speculate about the answers to some of the questions that form a vital part of this mystery. The first and most obvious question is, why was the prisoner masked? Surely we can rule out the idea that he was masked simply to hide some disfigurement; the fact that he was also isolated and forbidden to speak shows that there was more to it than that. Therefore we must assume that he was forced to wear a mask because he would be instantly recognisable. Yet nobody well-known had disappeared; so presumably he looked like somebody famous. But he could not have been masked *just* because he looked like somebody. Looking like somebody is not a punishable offence. He had spent the previous thirty years wandering at liberty with the same features, so obviously his facial likeness only became important in the context of his crime. Whatever he said or did was made doubly embarrassing to the authorities *because* he looked like somebody.

As to who that 'somebody' was, the most obvious guess is the king. The king took a deep interest in the prisoner, even going so far as to have lies spread about the case; the masked man was a royal guest, imprisoned without trial on the king's orders, in the king's prisons. Rumours of the royal connection abounded – that the prisoner was in fact the real king, or a twin imprisoned since birth. If the masked man did indeed resemble the king, it would explain why his captors were worried about him being recognised after thirty years in a mask: not because anybody would remember his face after so long, but because the similar features of the king had aged in the same way. It has even been suggested that some kind of switch was made in 1669, and an impostor substituted for the real monarch; but the king came into such close contact with hundreds of people every day (most notably his many mistresses) that a switch of this kind would have been impossible to pull off.

This leads us on to the question of who the masked man really was, and why he was treated so well within the confines of his imprisonment. If his secret was so momentous, why was he not killed? If his face was such an embarrassment, why was it not deliberately disfigured to obscure his identity? Whatever it was that the masked prisoner had done, he certainly seemed to expect death himself. The reason behind this royal compassion must be that the masked man was either a relative or a close friend of the king; presumably a relative, if there was indeed a facial resemblance. Yet no relatives of the king went missing; meaning that if he *was* a relative, the link must have been a secret one.

The fact that he was well-treated would seem to support the idea that he had once been an important, or at least comfortably placed person. He could obviously read and write, because searches were made for hidden messages; he seems to have been healthy enough, and he lived to a reasonable age. This was no peasant, but a member of affluent society. And yet no member of society had suddenly disappeared. From this evidence we must conclude that our prisoner, unless he was a recluse of the most secretive kind, had once held a position in society, but had lost it and dropped out of sight by the time of his arrest. In confirmation of this is the extraordinary fact that he never complained, threw tantrums, or seemed to have any desire to return to his former life; he appears to have accepted his lot quite contentedly. Unlike Fouquet and most other important prisoners, his imprisonment was hardly a matter of public knowledge; he had disappeared without trace, obviously never to return, so there was nothing to be gained by good behaviour. Therefore his extraordinary resignation to his fate must indicate that he had nothing to go back to. Either he had no family, they had disowned him, or they had been paid off in some way – remember that his imprisonment 'harmed no-one but himself'. Whatever position of eminence he had held was now permanently lost.

As to his crime, it would be hard to imagine a crime so terrible in itself that it had to remain secret for ever. Surely it was the masked man's secret, not his crime, that led him to his awful fate. Of course, if there was a crime, the gaol sentence would also act as punishment, but it is his secret that must have been the more provocative. It is not unreasonable to speculate that the two were connected, that he had tried to use the secret as part of a crime. Either he had always known the secret, but only now had misused it, or he had just discovered it and tried to misuse it. The third and non-criminal possibility is that he had been imprisoned simply because he had found out the secret; but as there were members of the government in the know as well, his imprisonment seems to indicate that his character was not to be trusted or had led him astray.

Whatever the secret was, it was a political secret of the greatest importance, as demonstrated by the cover-up operation and by the fact that it was entrusted to the minister of war's personal care under the direction of the king. It was also a royal secret of personal significance, that could be expected to cause great pain to the son of Louis xv. Louis xv lived from 1710 to 1774, which means that he did not have a son to refuse to tell until well over half a century after the masked man's arrest, when all the protagonists were long dead. So the secret must have been an enduring one, perhaps to do with the whole Bourbon dynasty, perhaps bound up with the secret relationship of Louis xiv to his masked prisoner. Certainly it was important enough for the prisoner's name and crime to be withheld from prison records and denied to posterity.

Such is the speculation that can profitably be allowed at this stage in the investigation. To go further without more information might be self-defeating. But the salient facts of the case can now be summarised as follows:

1. The prisoner was born in the late 1630s, arrested some thirty years later – probably in 1669 – and died on 19 November 1703.

2. He was kept masked, under high security, and was forbidden to speak – he would be killed if he did so, as would anyone who tried to free him or learn his secret. He was buried under the false name Marchioly, his corpse desecrated, and his furniture and belongings destroyed.

3. He was always in the charge of one governor – St Mars – and his staff, going with him from gaol to gaol. War ministry records show that St Mars in fact governed four gaols: Pignerol (1665) Exiles (1681) Sainte-Marguerite (1687) and the Bastille (1698), where the masked man was imprisoned in the Bertaudière Tower.

4. His case was personally supervised for the king by the war minister of the day – variously Louvois (1666), Barbezieux (1691) and Chamillart (1701). It was not only a political secret but a potentially hurtful royal secret, which died with Louis xv.

5. He was apparently French, Catholic, much travelled, and a man of education, breeding and good health. He was treated correspondingly well but nobody well-known had disappeared at the time.

6. He never complained, and his imprisonment 'harmed no-one but himself'.

7. He was referred to in prison either as 'the ancient prisoner' or as 'La Tour'.

8. He had some connection with Fouquet, whose 'secrets he knew'.

9. Contemporary rumours were rife, especially on the Isle of Sainte-Marguerite, in the Bastille and en route, but none of the theories predating Louis xv (1723) were in fact correct.

The next step in the investigation is to fit these facts to one of the prisoners in St Mars' care at Pignerol in the late 1660s – a group that includes the Italian Mattioli – and then to fit that prisoner into the mysterious royal plot that is beginning to take shape. But other detectives have examined the same clues beforehand, and the extraordinary conclusions that they have come to must also be investigated. To each theory must be applied not only the test of whether it fits the facts outlined above, but also the test of common sense: is it a likely story?

8

The mad monk, and other clerics

Likely or not, the story of the abbot who tried to swindle the King of England is one of the most extraordinary aspects of this case. It was unearthed for our benefit by the late Monsignor Arthur Stapylton Barnes, Roman Catholic chaplain to Cambridge University. His abbot was hardly a real abbot, but an amateur spy; he had been promoted from the level of monk by King Louis XIV so that he could travel to England and insinuate himself into King Charles's court as a bogus astrologer. As a swindler he was to prove a failure. His name was the Abbot Pregnani[1], and we first hear of him in February of that eventful year, 1669, when the French Foreign Minister Lionne wrote to his London embassy with news of their new agent.

> You are no doubt aware who Father Pregnani is. He is a Theatine [monk] whom the King has taken from the cloister and made an abbot. You will know also that he has as perfect a knowledge of judiciary astrology as is possible in a science that is so uncertain, and by its means he has got a great name here in Paris, especially among the ladies who are always curious about the future and want to know their fortune ... It is not impossible that the king of England may be persuaded on astrological grounds, since he puts much faith in them, that his only good and sure alliance is with France, and that any other entanglement may ruin his affairs and

his authority . . . [Pregnani] will not dare to fail, if he does not want to ruin himself.

King Louis had prepared the ground for his scheme by introducing the abbot to the Duke of Monmouth, Charles's son, who was visiting Paris at the time and who proceeded to invite the abbot to London. But Louis had not been cunning enough this time, for King Charles had already been tipped off about the fake astrologer by his sister Henrietta, Duchess of Orléans, who was variously Louis' cousin, sister-in-law, lover and mother to his child.[2] Charles wrote to her in reply:

I find your friend, the Abbot Pregnany, a man very ingenious in all things I have talked with him upon, and I find him to have a great deale of witt, but you may be sure I will enter no farther with him than according to your [report of his] carracter.

Charles was careful to steer conversation with the spy away from such sensitive topics of the time as the treaty of Dover, or his own Roman Catholic leanings. Indeed, once the hapless abbot had made some sort of name for himself in London society, without actually learning anything, he was lured by Charles to the Newmarket races and forced to use his 'astrological powers' to pick the winners. His newfound patron, the Duke of Monmouth, backed them all and lost his shirt. Not a single horse won. The abbot's public humiliation complete, he returned to France in disgrace.[3]

It is here that Monsignor Barnes' theory comes into play. The failed agent, he points out, set out for France on 17 July 1669 and was never seen again. The year is significant as we know; and so is the month, because on 19 July St Mars was instructed by Minister Louvois to expect a new prisoner, who was to be arrested at Dunkirk. Add to that de Renneville's mention of an Italian priest in the Bastille, a curious reference to a priest in an official letter concerning the prisoners at Pignerol, and the fact that locked away in one of St Mars' cells was a mad monk, and you have the makings of a real mystery.

You also have some easy targets to knock down. First, there is absolutely nothing to identify de Renneville's abbot, who was an Italian, with a French secret agent. Secondly, the mad monk in St Mars' care was not imprisoned until 1674; the prisoner arrested in Dunkirk was probably captured soon after 28 July 1669, five years too early to be the mad monk, but still some weeks after Pregnani set out for Paris. Even in the days before the invention of the cross-channel ferry it did not take more than a couple of days to get from London to Dunkirk. Then there is the question of why he should ever have become the masked man. The supposition that a failed spy who knew all the secrets of top-level diplomatic negotiations should be imprisoned to shut him up is not unreasonable, but why should he be masked? And why would he still be as fiercely guarded after thirty-four years? Why would long-exhausted diplomatic intrigue disturb – let alone upset – the king's great-great-grandson, well into the next century?

In fact there is little evidence to suggest that the masked man could have been a priest at all. He was not given a breviary[4], prayer books or any special priestly privileges, nor did anybody directly state anywhere at any time that he was a man of the cloth. It has been suggested that his quiet, uncomplaining demeanour was that of a monk or an abbot, but in fact religious prisoners usually made a lot of noise, ever convinced of their own righteousness. Besides, this society monk went to the racetrack! At any rate, one piece of evidence would seem to damn the case against the Abbot Pregnani. The memoirs of Primi Visconti, which Barnes did not see before forming his theory, distinctly mention the death of an abbot with this unusual name in Rome in the late 1670s. The abbot died 'completely rotted away with shameful diseases [that is to say, he died of syphilis], despite numerous horoscopes that were found on his table, in which he predicted that he would one day become Pope'.

The French writer, Marcel Pagnol, reluctant to drop the fascinating abbot from the picture, feels that Pregnani must have been only a go-between in the case; he believes that the masked man was in fact the rightful heir to the throne of France, waiting in England to lead a republican revolt in France, and that King Louis was unsuccessfully trying to arrange his extradition (before finally resorting to kidnap a few weeks later). He points out that the abbot ferried a letter from Charles to Louis, and that this was not the first time that mysterious messengers had been ferrying letters to and fro across the Channel. On 20 January 1669 Charles had written to his sister Henrietta:

> I receaved your [letter] by the Italian whose name and capasity you do not know, and he delivred your letter to me in a passage, where it was so darke, as I do not know his face againe if I see him.

But the mere fact that Charles had received this curious letter and sent another to King Louis is hardly enough to show that extradition proceedings were afoot! Would Louis really apply for extradition – a formal process – through an agent as unreliable as the abbot? If a character so danger-ous as the true king of France were at large in England, would he use a drawn-out legal process at all? Would he wait until 1669 to try and get his man? And if – as Pagnol claims – King Charles wanted to use the republican plotters to overthrow Louis, would he too have waited so long? Would he be so foolhardy as to instigate an anti-royalist revolt in France, so soon after his father's execution by Oliver Cromwell, when all he had to do was to make public the fact that Louis xiv had no right to his throne? Why risk his man at the head of an armed insurrection? The theory contains more convoluted ramifications yet, as we shall see, but one thing is sure: the astrological abbot was not the man taken to Pignerol and clapped into gaol for a life sentence of silence.

However, the mad monk, who was incarcerated there in 1674, does bear more investigation, if only to rule him out

of our enquiries. A handful of letters about him still remain,
sent by Louvois to St Mars. They refer to a prisoner

> who, although obscure, is still a man of consequence . . .
> he is a notorious rascal, who in a very serious matter has
> abused [the confidence of] important persons . . . he
> must be treated harshly by you, and you must give him
> only those things which are absolutely necessary for
> existence, with no other solace whatsoever.

It is almost certain that this monk was another society
swindler, which may account for the confusion. In 1673
Louis xiv wrote to the Archbishop of Lyons about a fake
fortune teller; a Dominican monk who, to everyone's
embarrassment, had seduced the wife of a royal cousin, the
Count of Armagnac. Interestingly enough, it is Primi
Visconti once more who tells us about him: 'All the women
revolved around him . . . he ended up by being thrown into
prison as an imposter.' The monk's punishment was certainly severe, but in a more traditional bread-and-water
fashion than that of the masked man, as Louvois instructed
St Mars in April 1674:

> I was very glad to hear of the arrival of the prisoner
> brought to you by the Chevalier de St Martin. It is the
> wish of the king that he be treated most harshly: you
> must not allow him a fire in his room except in the case
> of great cold or illness, and you must give him no other
> nourishment than bread, wine and water, for he is a
> thorough rogue, who cannot be sufficiently ill-treated nor
> suffer as much as he deserves. However, you may allow
> him to hear Mass, taking care nevertheless that he is not
> given the opportunity to make himself seen, nor to give
> information about himself. His Majesty also consents
> that you shall give him a breviary and some books of
> prayer.

By Christmas the regime had relented; he was allowed
better food and a confessor, and shared a cell with another
prisoner, Dubreuil. As if to assist in proving that this was

not the masked man, one more letter written in 1676 shows that the authorities could not even remember who their mad monk was:

> I bid you inform me who is lodged with M Dubreuil, whom you say is so mad, giving me his name and the one under which he was brought to you; and send me a copy of the letter that was written to you to receive him, so that I can better fix in my mind who he is.

Louvois went on to tell St Mars, that should the monk make any trouble, he should be threatened into submission. Failing that, he added later, the monk could be 'corrected rigorously'. It was a far cry from the cosseted world of the man in the iron mask.

The oldest of the prisoners died in 1694, and as no further record exists of the ecclesiastical lunatic, the only prisoner unaccounted for, one can only suppose that it was he. It certainly sounds like him: St Mars had moved on, taking his masked man with him, and neither the new governor of Pignerol nor the authorities in Paris could remember who on earth it was that had died. Embarrassingly, they had to write to St Mars to find out:

> The Seigneur de Laprade reports [from Pignerol] that the oldest of your prisoners is dead and that he does not know his name. Since I have no doubt that you can remember it, I ask you to send it to me.

For the ecclesiastical record, it has been suggested that an Eastern clergyman was kidnapped and masked and given to St Mars' care: Michael Avedick, beloved patriarch of the Armenian church and leader of thousands of Armenians in Constantinople. The shameful abduction of Avedick was indeed carried out by the French, at the fanatical instigation of the Jesuits, who showed little toleration of other forms of Christianity; he was taken to the fortress of the seven towers, and then thrown into a windowless black dungeon up to his neck in water. The Armenians engineered his release, so he was kidnapped again, and this time imprisoned in the Catholic monastery of Mont St Michel in France.

This is all very well, except that Michael Avedick was kidnapped in 1706, three years after the death of the masked man; our old friend Etienne du Jonca records his entry into the Bastille. After horrific treatment he was released in 1710, by now a forcibly converted Catholic, bent, wrinkled, blinded and prematurely aged; he found a small flat on the Rue Ferou and died there in poverty a year later. Indeed the only 'evidence' to connect this withered old man with the masked prisoner is the extraordinary statement that 'Marchialy', the incorrect version of the name on the masked man's grave, can be rendered into Armenian as 'Mar Kialy' literally 'Saint Mickey'. Let us say that this is not exactly a major piece of evidence for anything.

Of course it is still not impossible that the masked prisoner was a clergyman, but it has hardly been a profitable line of enquiry so far. But what has emerged from it are the curious comings and goings between England and France in that eventful summer of 1669, when a great number of people seem to have been scurrying to and fro on mysterious business. This is one of the major factors in the next great theory about the man in the iron mask, the story of another confidence trickster who moved in royal circles, but with a great deal more success.

Notes on Chapter 8

1 The English word 'Abbot' has been used to translate the French word 'Abbé,' although the two do not exactly correspond.
2 She was also Charles's lover at one time. A remarkable lady!
3 Charles wrote to Henrietta: 'I came from Newmarket the day before yesterday. I believe [the Abbot] will give you some account of it, but not that he lost his mony on confidence that the starrs would tell which horse would winn . . . James beleeved him so much, as he lost his mony upon the same score.'
4 A book containing the divine office of the Roman Catholic church for each day, carried by Catholic priests.

9

The man who fooled Rome

On 11 April 1668 a new recruit arrived at the house of Novices of the Jesuits, situated in the monastery of St Andrea in Rome. To say that the Jesuit brothers were surprised and delighted at their new arrival would be an understatement. They were astonished. His name meant little – 'James de la Cloche, of the island of Jersey under the King of England' – but the documents that he carried with him were pure political dynamite. They claimed not only that James was an unknown illegitimate son of King Charles II of England, but that Charles had decided to become an official Roman Catholic. Charles – the head of the most powerful Protestant nation in the world – ready to embrace Catholicism, and here was the man specifically charged to do the job! So pleased were the Jesuits, that they forgot to check or even question the young man's credentials.

Whether or not James was telling the truth, he certainly had his political facts right. What is more open to doubt is whether or not he had managed the incidental details correctly. All the detailed political knowledge in the world will not help an impostor if he doesn't speak the right language, or if his personal facts and references are wrong. Luckily for James de la Cloche, the Jesuits were so excited to discover him that they never stopped to ask themselves whether or not he really was the son of the King of England. But it is a question that we are at liberty to sit back and ask ourselves now.

James claimed to have been conceived in Jersey twenty-five years before, when Charles was in fact only 13, and to have been brought up in France. This, he explained, was why he spoke no English, only French and some Italian. In fact he signed his name in Italian, 'Giacomo della Cloche manna propria', which soon gave way to 'Giacomo Stuardo', making use of the royal family name of Stuart. He had never met his father, he said, until a visit to London in 1665, when the king had seen and recognised his teenage son, and had immediately charged him to go to Rome and negotiate his conversion to Catholicism.

James carried three letters to support these claims. One, written in Latin and signed by Queen Christina of Sweden in Hamburg in 1667, confirmed that Charles had acknowledged the Catholic James as his son, and said that James was 'designedly passing under the cognito of de la Cloche de Bourg'. The other letters, written in French, purported to come from Charles himself, and their veracity can now be examined carefully:

Given at Whitehall, 27 September 1665. Written and signed by our own hand, sealed with the ordinary seal for our letters without any addition. Charles.

Charles, by the Grace of God, King of England, France,[1] Scotland and Ireland, take for our natural son James Stuart, who by our order and command has lived in France and other countries under an assumed name up to the year 1665, when we took care of him; since the same year, he being in London, we of our express will and for just reasons have commanded him to live under this other name, that is: DE LA CLOCHE DU BOURG DE JERSEY, and for important reasons regarding the peace of the realm, we forbid him to speak of this until after our death. At that time he will then be permitted to present to Parliament our declaration, which for my own accord and with all fairness we have given to him at his request, in his own language to remove every excuse for his showing it to any person to be interpreted.

Another letter to the Jesuits, supposedly from Charles, also tried to sidestep the curious fact that the king of England was not writing in English:

> We are speaking in French to you, common to all persons of quality, and we believe that your most Holy Father knows it, rather than in poor Latin, which we can only employ in speech. Our principal aim in this is that no English be put under his nose for him to have to interpret.

The king then goes on to try and explain why he needs James or even the Jesuits to arrange his Catholic conversion:

> Although there are a multitude of [Catholic] priests here, such as are in the service of the two Queens,[2] with a party in each of our palaces of St James and of Somerset . . . at the same time we cannot make use of one because of the suspicion that we would create in our court through the conversation of these men . . . We cannot employ anyone else for this but him [James], who will always be sufficiently capable to administer to us in secret the sacraments of confession and Holy Communion that we wish to receive as soon as possible. This our son is a young cavalier, whom we know that you have received among you in Rome, under the name of the Sieur de la Cloche de Jersey, for whom we have always had a particular affection, because he was born to us when we were little more than sixteen or seventeen years old, of one of the most distinguished young ladies in our realm, more through our youthful frailty than wickedness; and also because of the natural excellence that you have [no doubt] always noticed in him.

James lived well in Rome at the Jesuits' expense, but perhaps they wanted to see more concrete evidence of his station in life; for another letter from London arrived, addressed this time to the 'Prince Stuart':

You must consider that we intend to recognise you publicly as our son within a few years; but neither Parliament nor business in general are well disposed to do that just at present . . . moreover, you must consider that you are in a position to claim similar titles on our behalf to those of the Duke of Monmouth, and perhaps even more; and moreover that we are without a child by the Queen, that those of the Duke of York[3] are very weak, and that by all logic and the quality of your mother you can claim to be preferred to the Duke of Monmouth by me and by Parliament . . . the Kingdom will belong to you, and Parliament cannot lawfully oppose it, except on the grounds that liberty of conscience is not restored and that, therefore, you as a Catholic cannot succeed, since all Kings must, as at present, be Protestants.

It is clear from these letters that 'King Charles' was extremely prolific. Whenever confidence in James seemed on the point of waning, another royal missive would pop up out of the blue. The letters assured all kinds of help, anytime, anywhere; they promised great endowments and the founding of abbeys; but only as long as nobody wrote to England directly. All correspondence had to be channelled through James. Always charming, the young noviciate predicted great things on the international stage, but spent most of his time borrowing huge advances. Not to worry, he told the Jesuits. Everything would be repaid at an interest rate of 1000 per cent.

Having heard James's story, it is not difficult to destroy the theory that he was really Charles's son, and later, the man in the mask. Enough evidence exists to expose the letters as forgeries: for James (or whoever wrote them) had not done his homework well enough. In the first place James claimed to be 24, which would mean that he was born in 1644. But Charles did not go to Jersey until 1646, and anyway would have been an extremely young father at 14.

Then there is the first letter of recommendation from

Charles, which is dated 27 September 1665, from Whitehall. But in the summer of 1665 the great plague was raging
in London, and Charles had taken his entire court away
from Whitehall, to Oxford. And there are other little
mistakes that the real Charles would never have made. He
would never have promised the throne of England to an
illegitimate son, or even suggested it, for that was expressly
forbidden by law. Conversely, he would never have said
that the law forbade kings to be Catholic – because it
didn't, until 1689. A Catholic king would certainly have
been frowned upon, even deposed, but it was not constitu-
tionally illegal to become one. Neither would Charles have
referred to a real son as 'The Prince Stuart'. He was careful
never to refer to any of his illegitimate sons by the title
'Prince' or 'Stuart'. This Charles, too, thought that his
mother was in England – the real Charles would have
known that she had left to live in France in 1665. Even the
royal handwriting on James's letters was wrong.

And on a more general note, Charles's weak excuse for
writing in French, his reasons for leaving the matter of his
conversion to James, his refusal to be contacted, and most
of the dates involved make little sense. Why did James
supposedly wait three years, from his commission to con-
vert Charles in 1665, before finally going to Rome in 1668?
And if he was born in Jersey, where was his mother in all
this? Who was she? Barnes produced a mother – Marguerite de Carteret, a young lady who could have known King
Charles as a boy. She married a Jean de la Cloche, the only
suitable de la Cloche on the island; but they only married
in 1657, which would make James no older than 11 by the
time he arrived in Rome in 1668. Unless of course Jean de
la Cloche was happy to claim the fatherhood of a boy
conceived thirteen years before he met and wed the
unmarried mother. If this was so, and James was born in
1644 as he claimed, he would still have been too young to
be the masked man. And anyway, why on earth should any
illegitimate son of Charles be such a great secret? He was

the unashamed father of several others, all very well known faces, such as the Dukes of Monmouth and St Albans.

The whole thing reeks of a gigantic swindle. Goodness knows how long James could have managed to string it out, had not Queen Christina of Sweden put the cat among the pigeons: because in the winter of 1668, she decided to pay a surprise visit to the Jesuits in Rome. It was Queen Christina who had allegedly signed the certificate verifying James's identity in the first place; and if the matter cropped up in conversation during her visit, some nasty questions might be asked. Quick as a flash, another letter from 'Charles' arrived:

> Although the Queen of Sweden is very sage and prudent, at the same time it is enough that she is a woman to make me believe that she can't keep a secret; and as she thinks she alone knows of the birth of our beloved son . . . your most Holy Father must avow to her that you have no knowledge whatsoever of his birth, in the event that she asks him.

There was only one thing for it. The letter might delay matters, but it would be safest for James to do a bunk. Apologising that his great conversion to Catholicism would have to be 'reserved for another occasion', 'Charles' announced that he wanted James to return to England:

> We beg [the Holy Father] herewith to send to us at once our most dear and beloved son . . . we believe that your most Holy Father has too much respect for crowned heads not to agree to such a just request.

Again at 'Charles's' request, James was excused the customary Jesuit escort. Borrowing £800, which the Jesuits never saw again, de la Cloche left for London at the turn of 1668/9, under the alias of 'Henry de Rohan', and disappeared.

The Catholic historian Monsignor Barnes, who advanced the Abbot Pregnani as a candidate for the masked prisoner, thought that James and his abbot were one and the same;

for James disappeared in the same year as the hapless abbot, and Barnes came to believe that James switched identities as a disguise. Another historian, Andrew Lang, takes the same view. The reason the French imprisoned and masked him, they say, is that as a go-between for Charles and his sister Henrietta in France, he simply knew too much. Important political negotiations were going on at that time, which eventually resulted in the Treaty of Dover in 1670[4] and James could not be left at liberty to use his knowledge of these negotiations.

The most recent idea on this matter, by the French writer Marcel Pagnol, accepts that James's letters were forgeries; but returns in desperation to the old 'unwanted twin' theory, making James de la Cloche the secret twin son of Louis XIII, who was only pretending to be the son of Charles II (the reason for which is not obvious). According to Pagnol, after the birth of the unwanted twin, the royal midwife brought up the child as she went about her midwifery duties; and when in England to assist with the birth of Charles's sister Henrietta, she deposited her little twin with the Carteret family in Jersey (we are not told why). This accounts for James's excellent French, ignoring the fact that he claimed to have lived in France and also the fact that as a Channel Islander he should have known some English.

Louis XIV, meanwhile, is hopping mad, and desperate to get his hands on his brother so that he can clap him in a mask; but Charles, we are told, sees his chance to undermine France by starting a republican revolt, with twin brother at the head. He fetches James from Rome, where he is inexplicably staying, and sends him to visit sister Henrietta in Paris so that she can verify his likeness to Louis – hence the exchange of mysterious Italian go-betweens. Without explaining why Charles would risk his valuable protégé in France, Pagnol assures us that James then left for London, set out for Paris again, and was kidnapped by Louis' men in the summer of 1669.

Although this confusing theory has the advantage over Barnes' original that we are not left trying to fathom out why Charles's illegitimate son should still be masked in prison two decades after his father's death, in all other respects it is complete gobbledegook. Fortunately for us, James himself comes to our rescue at this point, by revealing his whereabouts. For while James de la Cloche du Bourg, a.k.a. Henry de Rohan, a.k.a. Prince Giacomo Stuardo 'disappears' early in 1669, on the way to London, a familiar-sounding character crops up in Naples, calling himself 'Prince Giacomo Henry de Bovere Roana Stuardo'. This 'James' arrived in 1669, claiming to be an English prince on a rest cure, and busily throwing money around like confetti; he seduced, made pregnant and wed the daughter of Signor Corona, a local notable, whom he mollified with an enormous dowry. In fact he had so many hundreds of pounds to spend that he was arrested for forgery by the Spanish viceroy.

It was the end of the road for James. Claiming to be the illegitimate son of Charles II, he urged the viceroy to contact the Jesuits in Rome for confirmation; but the Spaniard went one better and contacted Charles himself, thus alerting the astonished English king to the presence of his supposed son for the first time. Charles promptly disavowed the whole matter and assigned a British agent, named Kent, to investigate. The viceroy proposed to have James horsewhipped through the streets of Naples, but the influential Signor Corona intervened to stop him, no doubt in the expectation of further financial reward. But James's money had run out. He died penniless in early September, leaving enormous sums that never materialised to his new family, along with the title of Marquis of Juvigny, worth a staggering £300,000 a year. Of course, there was no such title:

'And that', reported agent Kent, 'is the end of that Princely Cheate, or whatever he was.'

To this day, the Jesuits refuse to believe that they were tricked. James's son, born after his death, who had been promised the Principality of Wales or the Duchy of Monmouth, couldn't believe it either. He trailed around Italy and Germany for many years, claiming to be the rightful heir to the English throne, recognised officially by the Pope but by precious few others, before disappearing from sight in about 1750.

Barnes and Lang had no knowledge of James's short but spectacular second career when they formulated their theory about the man in the iron mask; but Marcel Pagnol, who seems to have included absolutely everything under the sun in one theory, explains it away by saying that by now, James the unwanted twin had swapped identities again, with a valet. He was now in London, pretending to be Martin, the valet of Roux de Marsilly, head of Charles's exiled French rebels. Why this should be so is not clear either.

Nonetheless, one man was arrested in Dunkirk in the summer of 1669 and taken to Pignerol, before James de la Cloche died in Naples. And that man was described, in one of the letters committing him to prison, as a valet. As the only one of St Mars' prisoners to be arrested in or around the significant year of 1669, it is a lead worth pursuing. And there are others beside Monsieur Pagnol who have seen some link between this man and the revolutionary conspirators led by Roux de Marsilly and his valet Martin, men who were definitely part of the heavy two-way traffic between England and the continent in that curious summer . . .

Notes on Chapter 9

1 A rather unrealistic conceit of the British royal family at the time.
2 Charles's wife Catherine and his mother Henrietta.
3 Charles's younger brother, who succeeded him as James II in 1685.
4 A treaty by which Charles guaranteed to help the French army in Holland if the French would support his ambitions as a Catholic.

10

The valet and the revolutionary

Paul Roux de Marsilly was publicly broken at the wheel, for conspiring against the life of King Louis XIV, on 26 June 1669. It wasn't a kind of rack. It literally meant being pounded to death by two huge men with an enormous wheel, in front of a baying crowd. Marsilly left behind him in London the shreds of an ambitious conspiracy – the 'League of Protestant states against France', a project that should have led him into Paris at the head of an army, not bound and gagged by the French snatch squad who had kidnapped him in Switzerland. He also left behind his valet, Martin, another man whom the French authorities were exceedingly anxious to interview.

It is doubtful whether the French really had anything to worry about. Roux de Marsilly and his small band of exiles had planned to invade France with the help of the Swiss, Spanish and Dutch armies. True, he had been intending to pay them well, by hiving off huge areas of France to them, but he was expecting them to conquer the areas in the first place. And with a network of spies as efficient as those of Louis XIV against him, Roux's plans never even approached fruition. For there was a traitor in his very own camp, an Englishman named Sir Samuel Morland. Morland invited the other plotters to dinner, but unknown to them he had hidden one of Louis' men, Ruvigny, in a secret cabinet before the meal. Ruvigny reported:

I have been in a secret place, from where I saw the man
[Roux] and heard his discourse, which made the hairs
on my head stand on end . . . I was in a cabinet, where I
could see him and hear him clearly at my ease, having
pen and paper to write down all that I heard him say.

King Louis put a price on Roux's head – one third of a
million pounds – and demanded his extradition. The
British held back. They wanted to see which way events
turned before committing themselves to either side, so Lord
Arlington told the French that the revolutionary had left
London. But Louis was too well informed to be deceived
for long. As Roux fled London for the continent in fear of
his life, Louis' men soon caught up with him.

It is now that the theory which makes his valet Martin
the man in the iron mask comes into play. For Roux was
put to torture, and under torture he began to ramble.
Exactly what he said is not known, but he seems to have
implicated Martin, because soon the French were after him
too. But Martin went to ground in London with his family,
and refused to emerge. The French tried extradition again;
they even offered Martin cash to give evidence against
Roux. All apparently unsuccessfully. Martin remained
where he was. But not for long, say Messrs Iung, Barnes,
Lang and Pagnol, four of the major investigators who have
tried to unravel the mystery. Not only was it Martin who
was hunted down and arrested at Dunkirk in the late
summer of 1669, they say, but according to the latter three
historians, the man in the iron mask was also variously
James de la Cloche and the Abbot Pregnani, who were all
one and the same man. And according to Pagnol he was
also the King of France's identical twin brother.

On their side is the reference of St Mars having a valet
for a prisoner. Against them is not only enough evidence to
acquit Martin of whatever crimes the masked man may
have committed, but almost enough evidence to try them
instead for libelling him. Most damning are two letters. In
the first, the French ambassador to London, Colbert, wrote

to his government: 'I will send him [Martin] to you if he can be of any use: unless you order me to let him go.' On 13 July, Foreign Minister Lionne replied: 'After the execution of Roux it will no longer be necessary to make Martin come to France.' Does this sound as if it refers to a prisoner so important that he had to be shut away and covered up for life? Or does it seem to refer to an unimportant valet?

But assume for the moment that Martin really was a man in possession of some vital fact, some piece of information so important that he had to be locked up for ever. Assume, even, that he was the king's twin brother. Why, then, would the French bother to offer him money to come to France, when he would obviously refuse? Why would they execute Roux de Marsilly in public, when he might blurt out the same amazing fact about Martin that he had told his interrogators? Why didn't Martin ever try to use his amazing piece of information? If he was caught and imprisoned, why did his family never complain from the safety of their foreign shore? And if he was the man hunted down and arrested in Dunkirk, why had he gone to France at all? He would not have gone voluntarily, as he made clear; yet logically, if he had gone under duress, he would not have needed to be hunted down. Surely, Martin was simply a valet who knew nothing except what his master Roux had been up to. As he said himself, he did not want to be 'kept in prison to make him divulge what he did not know'.

There is absolutely no evidence that Martin the valet ever left England. Furthermore, we know that the masked man was a Roman Catholic. Yet Martin was part of the 'League of Protestant states against France'. If he was just a Protestant valet, there would be no point in covering his face and keeping him alive at great expense. But if 'Martin' was only a false name, one of several, why bother to give him yet another name? Why not keep up the pretence that he was Martin the valet, imprisoned for joining a Protestant republican plot?

The exploits of Martin, James de la Cloche and Pregnani have provided the basis of the main 'alternative' theories about the man in the mask. But, like the traditional theory and the official versions of the story, they have proved seriously lacking. They can be exposed on technical points, such as dates and times, and also on grounds of common sense. And, if this is not too fanciful, they actually *feel* like digressions from the main story, like mere flirtations with the peripheral characters of 1669. None of these revolutionaries, confidence tricksters, spies or messengers has a solid air of importance; they have crept into the reckoning by virtue of being intriguing and mysterious.

They are not alone in their candidacy; many other investigators have put forward their own men, most of whom are worth only the briefest mention. There was General Bulonde, punished (for raising a siege on his own initiative) with a ten-year spell in Pignerol, after the gaoler St Mars had departed; but receipts signed by him have been found, dated 1699 and 1705. There was Louis Oldendorff, another candidate of the historian Iung, a spy and poisoner arrested in 1673 and taken to the Bastille; but this idea rested only on the fact that Oldendorff had relatives called Malatour, and Mareshal, and the family name de Marcheuille, names which recall the 'Marchioly' buried in 1703. There was Loquin's absurd theory that Molière, the playwright who died in February 1673, was really kidnapped by Jesuits, who didn't like his play 'Tartuffe', and taken to the Bastille. There was the common suggestion that the minister Fouquet became the masked man, even though he died in 1680 at Pignerol in the presence of his whole family, and even though he would have been 88 by 1703. And there was Marshal Catinat, a mysterious prisoner at Pignerol who has since turned out to have been a government agent in disguise.

A popular candidate was the Count of Vermandois, High Admiral, who appeared thinly disguised as the masked man in the anonymous satire, *The History of Persia*. Vermandois was the much loved son of Louis XIV and his first mistress Louise de la Vallière, and died after a long illness at the siege of Courtrai in 1683. Quite apart from the fact that he was only two in 1669, his dead body was clearly borne through the streets of Arras in 1683 in a four-day public funeral ordered by the grief-stricken king. According to the book, he was imprisoned for striking the dauphin, but as both were young boys at the time, it is difficult to see how anyone would have minded.

Another historian, Pierre Vernadeau, claimed that the masked prisoner was the son-in-law of a royal physician, who had discovered proof in his father-in-law's papers that King Louis XIII was impotent. Monsieur Vernadeau offered no explanation for the mask or for the continued survival of his candidate. Camille Bartoli's 1978 book, 'I discovered the incredible secret of the iron mask', postulated a secret plot to restore the line of King Clovis (whose descendants had been deposed a thousand years before) in the shape of the Duke of Guise, who would in fact have been approaching a hundred in 1703.

Jean Christian Petitfils, writing in 1970, accused Louvois of imprisoning his own valet, after hiring him unsuccessfully to carry out a murder – again, no explanation for the mask – while Count Michel de la Cour, although lacking a brilliant theory of his own, insisted that he had found the skeleton of the masked man in his house in Cannes in 1978.

But perhaps the most entertaining of all, and very much the last theory worthy of mention, is that advanced by the Emperor Napoleon, who investigated the story after the revolution, with the help of Talleyrand. Napoleon decided that the masked man was indeed the rightful heir to the throne of France, and that Louis XIV was an impostor. He explained that the prisoner had been allowed to settle down on the island of Sainte-Marguerite and raise a family. As the child of a king, the son had been named 'Good Stock', which – because the island was quite near Italy – translated into the Italian 'Buona-Parte'. Which, of course, is Napoleon's surname. The rest, unhampered by a complete lack of evidence of any kind, is not difficult to guess.

You may judge for yourself the accuracy and likelihood of these stories. If you are convinced that the masked man was really an Italian confidence trickster monk valet who found political intrigue too complicated to manipulate, or if you believe in any of the other possibilities outlined above, read no further. But the key to this mystery lies surely in the prisons and fortresses of Louis xIV's France, and in the prisoners who are known to have been in the charge of the gaoler St Mars. It is time to leave the outside world of diplomatic intrigue and political plots, and enter the great gates of the citadel of Pignerol.

11

Behind fortress walls

High in the Southern Alps, perched on a mountain commanding the old road to France, lies the small Italian town of Pinerolo. Three hundred years ago it was the mighty fortress of Pignerol, marking the furthest extent of French territory. It was also an excellent place in which to hide a prisoner. A double line of thick walls marked the boundaries of the citadel, punctuated with four high towers, which commanded a view for miles in every direction. Soldiers patrolled the walls regularly and one was stationed at the base of each tower, inside and out. Around the outer wall was a wide moat. Within the citadel lay another line of defence; the high walls of the keep, drawbridge raised in isolation from the citadel outside, with its two towers. Each tower had three floors, with one large room on each floor. Each room was self-contained, and the whole was overlooked by the governor's apartment. Of the two towers, the lower was the more secure – 'La tour d'en bas', as it was known, or 'La tour' for short. It was this tower that lent its nickname to its masked inhabitant.

Discreetly as security was maintained at the fortress, the fearsome reputation of Pignerol spread throughout France. When the Count of Lauzun heard that he was to be taken there, he tried to kill himself. But not all of the fear that the name aroused stemmed from the prison itself. For the gaoler of Pignerol, St Mars, was the ideal man to guard a prisoner that you never wished to see again. Nobody ever escaped St Mars. Cringing and deferential to his masters, his subservience vanished inside the walls of his fortress. Constantin de Renneville, his prisoner in the Bastille, gave us this description:

> He was a little man, very thin, his head, hands and all his body shaking, and received us very courteously. He held out his shaking hand to me and put it into mine. It was as cold as ice, which made me say, within myself, 'This is an ill omen; death, or its substitute, enters into alliance with me.' He was a very ugly little man, and ill-shaped, and looked to be near eighty years of age when I first saw him, bowed and shaking, swearing, and terribly hasty, swearing and blaspheming continually, and in appearance always in a passion, hard-hearted, inexorable, and cruel in the highest degree.[1]

Once, this shrivelled caricature had been a dashing young musketeer. In those days, his name was Benigne Dauvergne. Born in 1626 and soon an orphan, he had grown up to fight with distinction in the saddle, reaching the rank of brigadier by 1660. He was part of the carefree, swashbuckling generation of d'Artagnan and his friends, but not a natural part. His extraordinary devotion to duty – and his extraordinary devotion to money – had been noticed, and he was soon to leave the world of his youthful successes.

The turning point came in 1661, when Louis XIV charged the faithful d'Artagnan to arrest the minister Nicolas Fouquet, the rival whose downfall the king had plotted. D'Artagnan took St Mars as his second in command, and was obviously struck by the thoroughness and application that his deputy brought to the task. As the most important minister in France, Fouquet knew every secret there was to know, and would need to be kept well out of the way in the hands of one trusted man. D'Artagnan knew who the right man was, and recommended St Mars for the job. Four years later, when the trial of the century was over and Nicolas Fouquet had been sentenced by the king to life imprisonment, d'Artagnan and a hundred of his musketeers escorted Fouquet to his new home at Pignerol, and delivered him into the hands of his new master St Mars.

St Mars was to prove an excellent gaoler, even better than Louis XIV and d'Artagnan had hoped. He supervised the treatment of his prisoners personally; he never missed the tiniest detail; he sent assiduous reports; he was eager to please. Around him he appointed only men he could trust, such as his relatives the de Formanoirs, and his cousin Blainvilliers from the family who had raised him when his parents died. Little did St Mars know it, but he was being groomed for a more important prisoner than Nicolas Fouquet.

It was into this atmosphere of suspicious, watchful security that the masked prisoner was introduced; and even the assiduous precautions of St Mars were tightened up for the new arrival. Any stranger who stopped to look at the citadel for even a moment was arrested and interrogated. The governor of the citadel, de Pienne, who considered the prison governor St Mars a social upstart, should have been his superior; but he was specially ordered by the minister of war, Louvois, to put himself at St Mars' disposal. Anything St Mars wanted, de Pienne was to provide. And to cap it all, Louvois – who had been put in personal charge of the man in the mask – instituted his own little check. Unknown to St Mars, he placed a spy on the prison staff, to report on everything that happened at Pignerol.

The whole project – keeping this man safe, secure, comfortable and anonymous – cost Louis XIV the most staggering sum. Not only was he prepared to pay for extra solid walls and oak doors to keep his prisoner well locked in, but he was prepared to pay his gaolers handsomely into the bargain. St Mars' personal salary was gigantic. By 1698, the time of his move to the Bastille, he was earning £40,000 a year – and that at seventeenth-century prices. On top of this he received regular bonus payments for his successful work: £30,000 in November 1677, for example, and £15,000 in January 1679. It is worth bearing in mind that peasant workers at this time were receiving about £1 a week, soldiers about £2 a week. Considering that in 1698, £1 would buy you about three chickens, or perhaps 5lbs of butter (assuming you wished to spend your wages entirely on chickens or butter) then at a conservative estimate each pound was worth around £10 of today's money. In other words, St Mars' wages amounted to the equivalent of a million pounds every two and a half years. Add to that the three titles he received, plus the spectacular promotion of his family and his staff, then you realise that his loyalty cost the king no mean sum.

St Mars' sister-in-law, Mme Dufresnoy, was in fact the mistress of Louvois, but it is doubtful that this had anything to do with the gaoler's lavish rewards; this money came straight from the king. Louis spent large amounts on the prisoner too. For instance, when the masked man was moved to the Isles of Sainte-Marguerite, a special cell block was built for him at a cost of £7,200. In June 1681 we know that St Mars was getting £4,380 a year for his prisoner's upkeep, at a time when normal prisoners were receiving less than £25 per annum. The usual amount spent on the other prisoners at the Isles of Sainte-Marguerite was a pathetic 15 sous per day, while this man went through the equivalent, in today's money, of £900 a week – in a cell!

What Louis was buying, both from his prisoner and his gaoler, was acquiescence. The irony is that St Mars could never spend all his money; when he died, he still had virtually the whole sum in his possession. He was almost as much a prisoner as the man he was looking after. For thirty-four years he lived with him, served him, searched him, was often his only companion; and yet he was never actually allowed to talk to his prisoner about anything other than his basic needs. He was absolutely forbidden to learn anything. Looking back, it is impossible not to entertain a sneaking suspicion that St Mars must have discovered his prisoner's secret. If he genuinely never found out what that secret was, then curiosity must have eaten him away for thirty-four years. Yet if he did discover anything, we shall never know, because he would not have dared to admit it. He kept his mouth shut and made millions.

We owe these economic facts to one Bishop Massieu, who spent two decades after the revolution classifying the archives of the war ministry into 800 thick volumes for publication, without ever realising just what they contained. It is to these volumes that we must turn next, to discover what really passed behind the walls of the fortress of Pignerol. Louis and his Minister Louvois obviously thought that their secret would be safe, buried in the archives of the ministry; but even so they took precautions against the future, and destroyed nearly all the correspondence passing to and from St Mars, that related to the masked man. Luckily, about a hundred letters survive out of those they sent to the gaoler. The letters contain only a patchwork of odd references and clues, but just enough to build up a picture of our quarry.

It is from some of these letters that the facts relating to Louis' huge expenditure were drawn; and if the reader will forgive a further piece of advance editing, it would be useful to make a few observations as to their general drift, before examining them individually. They are vitally important documents. Not only do they make clear who was imprisoned in Pignerol at the time, but they demonstrate a number of extremely significant points.

First and foremost, they show a distinct interest in one prisoner, an interest displayed not only by the minister, but by the king himself. This one prisoner is clearly referred to as the 'ancient prisoner' by the time he is incarcerated on the Isles of Sainte-Marguerite; but at Pignerol, where all the prisoners were referred to by name, there is more than one candidate. So what must be decided is, which of the prisoners at Pignerol became the 'ancient prisoner'. For the 'ancient prisoner' as we know, was the name given to the man in the mask.

Secondly, and curiously, the letters show that security became tighter and precautions more rigorous as the years went by, rather than becoming more relaxed as one might expect. This is all the more unusual as the letters' third trend is that the 'ancient prisoner' always remained completely and utterly tranquil, never causing any trouble. Fourthly, it is noticeable that the king and his minister were always concerned for the welfare of their prisoner; they always asked after his health and wellbeing, while recommending with the same breath that other prisoners be savagely beaten. What kind of man was it that was kept alive and comfortable, but silent and invisible, at a cost of millions, where other men were treated like rats or executed on a whim? Life was certainly not the sort of privilege extended by the king to some of his ministers. Both Louvois and his successor at the ministry, his son Barbezieux, were almost certainly murdered when Louis felt he could no longer trust them with his great secret.

The bullish Marquis de Louvois has been described as 'a pitiless bully', 'the greatest brute that ever lived'. He was responsible for most of the French military atrocities of Louis' reign. But he was also loyal to his monarch, highly efficient, and a great administrator: the ideal man for Louis to trust to look after the masked prisoner. His father, Le Tellier, had been another of Louis' most trusted men. Exactly what led Louis to decide to dispose of him is unclear; but decide he did, and in July 1691 a warrant was issued to arrest Louvois and conduct him to the Bastille. The day before he was due to go, on the sixteenth, he was suddenly taken ill and died in brief agony. The court diarist St Simon tells us what happened:

> The sudden illness and death of Louvois caused plenty of gossip, especially so when it emerged from the autopsy of his body that he had been poisoned. He was a great water-drinker, and always kept a water jug on the mantelpiece in his room, from which he would drink. It was known that he had drunk some before leaving to go and work with the King; and that between the end of dinner with several people, and his entry into his room

to fetch the papers that he wanted to take to work with the King, a servant had entered his room and remained there alone for a few moment. [The servant] was arrested and thrown in prison; but he had been there scarcely four days, and proceedings had begun, when he was released by order of the King, that which already had been done was thrown upon the fire, and any further researches were forbidden. It even became dangerous to speak about it, and the family of Louvois stifled all its complaints, in such a manner as to leave no doubt that a very precise order had been given.

The second minister of war to take charge of the masked man, and whose name appears on the letters to St Mars, was Louvois' son, the Marquis de Barbezieux. Barbezieux was only 22 and Louis hoped to control him, but in the event was defeated by the young Marquis' laziness and debauchery. The king also complained of his rudeness and untruthfulness. Interestingly, he objected to Barbezieux's friendship with any of his own sons. After ten years in office, Barbezieux simply disappeared. Officially it was announced that, at the age of 33, he had been 'exhausted by his excesses'. In his palace, Louis and his close friends celebrated.

By this time the man in the mask had arrived at the Bastille in Paris, and the flow of letters had stopped. We know that Chamillart took over as minister of war, and as the watcher over the masked man, but little is known about his tenure of this dangerous post. Certainly, unlike normal military prisons, the Bastille was nothing to do with the ministry of war, but Louis made sure that the same minister had sole charge of his special prisoner, wherever he was.

Of all the guardians of the secret, only St Mars, and his two faithful henchmen Rosarges and Ru, remained impassively at their posts for the whole thirty-four years. It was more important for Louis to find an understanding gaoler than the right gaol. But ironically, the only officer who ever made a mistake, throughout the masked man's whole prison life, was St Mars. Solid, watchful, meticulous St Mars. There is one letter, amongst all the royal instructions and replies, that does not come from the ministry archives: a letter written by St Mars, without the knowledge of his superiors, to another government official, which contains a vital clue. It could be that this letter, discovered years later, is the one to bring down the whole of King Louis XIV's carefully constructed scheme.

That letter will follow in due course. But now is an appropriate time to examine the prisoners under St Mars' care at Pignerol and the letters dealing with them. Some prisoners came and went, and were seen again in the outside world; but there were six who entered the gates of the fortress and never saw the outside again. These six men are the ones that must be investigated, to determine which became the 'ancient prisoner', and 'man in the iron mask'. Two can be discounted immediately: the mad monk, of our acquaintance, gaoled in 1674 and dead by 1694, and a spy named Dubreuil, whose arrest in Alsace in 1676 and death in prison in 1697 are no secret. One more can be discounted, but has a further part to play in our story: Nicolas Fouquet, the Finance Minister, who as we know arrived at Pignerol in 1665 and died in 1680. The remaining three are our candidates. One is Hercules Mattioli, a double-crossing Italian diplomat, arrested in 1679. One is named La Rivière – he was Fouquet's valet. And the third is something of a mystery: a man named Eustache Dauger. No details are given about who he was, or what he had done. But – he was arrested in the summer of 1669.

Notes on Chapter 11

1 Renneville was also illuminating on the characters of many of St Mars' staff. Major Rosarges was covered in pustules, and had a taste for the bottle; de Formanoir was a shabby, shuffling man with little kindness in him; du Jonca was basically a good sort; Ru was likeable, but like Rosarges stole from the prisoners; Lecurjer

was a hunchback, bald, essentially a nice man; Giraut, the Chaplain, had a hook nose and an eye for the ladies; while Dr Reilhe was summed up as highly ambitious and concerned principally with looking after No. 1.

12

The double-dealing diplomat

Hercules Anthony Mattioli was arrested by French soldiers on 2 May 1679, and conducted to Pignerol. Originally, he had been an Italian university professor; but his mental agility had led him into politics, to the foreign secretaryship of Mantua, and from there via a complicated and unsuccessful bit of trickery into the inside of a French prison. His idea had been audacious – to fool the King of France and make some money into the bargain – and it nearly came off.

Mattioli's master, the Duke of Mantua, owned the fortress of Casale in Northern Italy, not far from Pignerol. Its strategic value made it a sought-after prize, and Louis xiv was always interested in buying it; in 1632 he had obtained Pignerol in a similar way. So it was that Mattioli approached the French ambassador in Venice, the Abbot d'Estrades, with the news that his master the duke wished to sell. In return for a suitable reward, he said, he would make sure that the duke sold Casale to France. The abbot relayed the news to Paris and Louis took the bait. The price of Casale was to be 100,000 crowns: Mattioli's 'commission' was to be a further 6,000 crowns, plus a huge diamond. The pay-off was made in secret at a masked ball at the Venice Carnival, so that the deal could be hidden from the Spanish, Venetian and other spies who were keeping their eyes open at the court; and Louis' agent, the Baron d'Asfeld, was sent to collect the document.

But now that Mattioli had the money, he acted quickly to double-cross the French and cut short the deal. Given advance warning, there were several interested parties who could move to stop the French taking Casale – the Venetians, Turinese and Milanese, the Spanish, the Austrians – and Mattioli let them all into the secret of the negotiations. Louis' man, the Baron, walked straight into a Spanish trap.

As far as Mattioli knew, it had worked like a dream. Unfortunately for him, however, he too had been outsmarted. One of the interested parties he had tipped off was Madame Royale, Duchess of Savoy; and although she was happy to stop the deal, she felt she should balance this by getting into Louis' good books, by betraying Mattioli to the French. So when Mattioli went in all innocence to a hastily convened meeting with Abbot d'Estrades, on French territory, he found himself being ambushed in turn and led away by French soldiers. King Louis XIV was not the easiest man to embarrass and then hope to get away with it.

In fact, by the time Mattioli was arrested, the plans for St Mars to receive him were already made. On 27 April 1679, Louvois had written to St Mars:

> The King has sent orders to the Abbot d'Estrades to try to arrest a man, with whose conduct His Majesty has reason to be dissatisfied: of which he has commanded me to inform you, so that you may not object to receiving him when he is sent to you; and so that you may guard him in such a manner that not only may he have no communication with anyone, but that also he may have reason to repent of his bad conduct, and that it may not be discovered that you have a new prisoner.

D'Estrades was told to send Mattioli to Pignerol. The king informed him, 'instructions are being sent to receive him and keep him there without anyone knowing about it.'

The troops that had arrested Mattioli were commanded by Marshal Catinat, who had been waiting with St Mars at Pignerol, ready to make his move, under the alias of

Monsieur Richemont. Catinat obviously enjoyed using false names, because he gave Mattioli the false name Lestang. This was his report:

> I arrested Mattioli yesterday, three miles from here, upon the King's territories, during an interview which the Abbot d'Estrades had ingeniously convened between him, Mattioli and myself, to facilitate the scheme. For the purpose of arresting him, I was only served by the Chevalier de Saint-Martin and de Villebois, officers of St Mars, and by four men of his company: it was effected without any violence, and no-one knows the name of this rogue, not even the officers who helped me to arrest him: he is in the room which the man named Dubreuil occupied, where he will be treated civilly, according to the request of the Abbot d'Estrades, until the wishes of the King upon the subject are known . . . I have rendered an account to Monseigneur of all that I have done there with Mattioli, to whom I have given the name Lestang, no-one knowing who he is.

Today Mattioli is the historians' 'official' candidate. This initial flurry of letters does contain some support for that idea: because it is quite clear from them that Mattioli's name was to be kept secret. 'No-one knows the name of this rogue', wrote Catinat, giving him a false name; 'without anyone knowing about it', ordered Louis. Furthermore, a pamphlet produced later in Italy said that Mattioli had been surrounded, masked and carried off by ten or twelve horsemen. Mattioli was the right age for our prisoner, born as he was in 1640. His name is similar to the masked man's grave-name, Marchioly; he was identified as the masked man by Louis xv to his mistress; and he was the only candidate King Louis xvi could come up with.

Against this are some even better arguments. Most important of all is the fact that Mattioli's arrest and imprisonment were no secret in Europe. The prison in which he was hidden had of course to be kept secret, in case his friends tried to cross the border and rescue him, but the very fact that he had been taken was intended to serve as a warning to others of the perils of double-crossing France. Full details of his crime and abduction were published in 1681, 1687 and 1749.[1] The Duke of Mantua knew full well what had happened to his errant minister. Mattioli was even made to write to his father, to tell him what had happened, and to instruct him to hand over incriminating papers.

Within Pignerol, too, Mattioli's conditions did not correspond with the incredible secrecy that later surrounded the masked man. The name 'Lestang' began to drop from use from 1680 onwards. Unlike the masked man, who was only to be seen by the governor and Rosarges, Mattioli was spied on by all St Mars' lieutenants; unlike the mask, who was to remain silent or be killed, Mattioli was interrogated to make him reveal all he knew; unlike the mask, whose health and standard of living were carefully preserved, Mattioli was given medicine only in cases of severe illness – his treatment was intended to make him 'repent of his bad conduct'; and unlike the mask, who was not allowed to write anything down, Mattioli was given pen and ink, according to letters of 1679, 'to put into writing whatever he may wish to say'. As to the pamphlet which described his arrest and masking, it was obvious that the details had been made up. There were not, for instance, 'ten or twelve horsemen'. There is absolutely no way that anyone would have been allowed to witness the scene and get away to write about it.

In addition to these anomalies are the general arguments that can be advanced against Mattioli. He was arrested in 1679, ten years too late. As we know, Lamotte-Guérin categorically put the date of the masked man's arrest at 1669, Antoine Ru's reference puts it between 1667 and 1672, and Barbezieux, writing to St Mars in April 1691, refers to him obliquely as 'the prisoner who has been in your custody for twenty years'. This is presumably a rough date, as the only prisoner at Pignerol arrested in 1671 was the Count of Lauzun, released ten years later and still alive in 1723. So only Eustache Dauger, arrested in 1669, fits the bill. Mattioli is rather too late. Furthermore the similarity of 'Mattioli' to 'Marchioly' and the testimony of Louis XV to a mistress (when he wouldn't tell his own son lest it cause him pain) surely point to the idea that Mattioli was actually being pushed forward as the official candidate, to cover up something else, and that later historians were taken in by this. Then of course there is the royal admission about the masked man that 'the imprisonment of this unfortunate person harmed no-one but himself'; hardly a remark that fits a man who had a wife, children and a secure home life. Mattioli was hardly an 'unfortunate person' either; he was an out and out criminal. And how on earth would the imprisonment of a crooked Italian diplomat have hurt the son of Louis XV half a century later? At this early stage, the case for Hercules Anthony Mattioli is looking rather unlikely.

On 6 May 1679, soon after his arrest, an old companion was provided for Mattioli. Marshal Catinat wrote to Louvois: 'D'Estrades has found means to send the servant of the Sieur de Lestang to Pignerol, with his goods and all his papers.'

This reference provides us with a clue that will come in useful later, when trying to identify our nameless prisoner: that Mattioli had a valet. Further clues come in the complaints of St Mars to Louvois about Mattioli's mental state, early in 1680:

The Sieur de Lestang has become like the monk in my care; that is to say, subject to fits of raving madness, from which the Sieur Dubreuil also is not exempt . . . The Sieur de Lestang, who has been nearly a year in my custody, complains that he is not treated as a man of his quality, and the minister of a great Prince, should be. Despite this, I continue to follow your commands upon this subject to the letter, as well as upon all others. I think he is deranged, by the way he talks to me, telling me that he talks every day to God and his angels; that they have told him of the death of the Duke of Mantua, and of the Duke of Lorrain [sic]; and, to verify this madness, he says that he has the honour to be a close relative of the King, to whom he wishes to write, to complain about the treatment that I give him. I have not thought it right to give him paper or ink for that purpose, seeing that he is not in his right senses.

Louvois wrote to St Mars:

With regard to the Sieur de Lestang, I admire your patience, and the fact that you waited for an order to treat this rascal as he deserves, when he fails to show you respect.

These letters do not seem to support the theory that Mattioli was the masked man. True, he claimed to be the relative of the king, but he also claimed to talk to God every day. And it was obvious that he was going to suffer for it. Mattioli was a 'rascal', not a pampered house guest.

Further proof that he was hardly a respected, important prisoner came on 16 August 1680, when St Mars actually received permission to put him with another prisoner. Louvois wrote:

I have seen, from your letter of the 7th of this month, the proposition that you make of putting the Sieur de Lestang with the Jacobin [monk], to avoid the necessity of two chaplains. The King approves that which you have suggested, and you have only to carry it out.

Much has been made of the curious reference to 'avoiding the necessity of two chaplains'. Those who believe that the masked man was a priest, maybe the Abbot Pregnani, think that this means there were two priestly prisoners: the mad monk, and another, the masked man. But no other prisoner was ever referred to or treated like a priest; surely it simply means that Mattioli and the monk could take confession at the same time, from the same chaplain, for convenience's sake. At any rate, the effects of putting the two together proved rather amusing, as St Mars reported on 7 September:

> Since you, Sir, permitted me to put Mattioli with the Jacobin in the Lower Tower, the said Mattioli was for four or five days in the belief that the Jacobin was a man that I had placed with him to watch his actions. Mattioli, who is almost as mad as the Jacobin, walked about with long strides, his cloak over his nose, saying that he was not a dupe; that he knew more than he would say. The Jacobin, who was always seated on his pallet, with his elbows leaning upon his knees, looked at him gravely, without listening to him. The Signor Mattioli remaining always convinced that it was a spy that had been given to him, was disabused, when one day the Jacobin got down from his bed stark naked, and began to preach, without rhyme or reason, till he was tired. I and my lieutenants saw all their manoeuvres through a hole over the door.

Note that the 'Sieur de Lestang' has already given way to the 'Signor Mattioli' in official correspondence, only sixteen months after his arrest. But note also, that Mattioli and the mad Jacobin monk are in one of the rooms of the lower tower. This is a point in Mattioli's favour, for it was from this tower that the masked man earned his nickname. The lower tower is an important point of reference, because when St Mars moved on to govern the fortress of Exiles in 1681, only two prisoners were considered important enough to go with him – two prisoners from the lower tower. All his prisoners rejoined him later at the Isles of Sainte-Marguerite, but – with the exception of Fouquet, who by this time was already dead – only the two from the lower tower actually stayed under his guard continuously until their deaths. Unfortunately for the Mattioli theorists, the diplomat and the monk were not the only pair of prisoners in the lower tower; it contained three rooms. But which two prisoners went to Exiles?

The letter transferring St Mars, written by Louvois on 12 May 1681, ran as follows:

> . . . the King has thought it proper to accord to you the Governorship of Exiles, where he will transport those of your prisoners under your [personal] guard, whom he thinks to be of such importance that they should not be entrusted to any other hands but yours. I have asked the Sieur Duchaunoy to come and visit all the buildings [at Exiles] with you, to make a record of the alterations absolutely necessary for their lodging. Send me a list of all the prisoners under your care, and mark for me, opposite that which you know of the reasons they were arrested. With regard to the two in the lower tower, you need only designate them by this name, without adding anything else.

Obviously, of the five men at Pignerol in 1681, these were the two prisoners of real importance. St Mars was not supposed to know their crimes. When Barbezieux referred to the masked man in 1691, he spoke to 'the prisoner who has been in *your* custody for twenty years', not in anybody else's custody while St Mars was at Exiles. And Duchaunoy, who became minister of fortifications, was directly ordered to go to Exiles to build a secure new cell for these two men: 'His Majesty desires that two of the prisoners who are under [St Mars'] guard to be transferred there, to be subject to as much security there as at Pignerol. You must not mention them in any way in [your] report.'

Eventually, the cell cost £6,000 and took forty-five guards three months to build. It was definitely no ordinary room. Soon afterwards, the transfer to Exiles took place. Louvois confirmed: 'The intention of His Majesty is that you transfer there the said two prisoners that I referred to in my last letter.'

But what is all this about *two* prisoners? Only one masked man died in 1703 – who was this fellow prisoner, when the man in the mask was allowed no companions? And was Mattioli one of the two? A suggestion that Mattioli was one of the pair comes in a rather convoluted episode, which all started back in October 1680, when St Mars wrote to Louvois and offered to send him Mattioli's ring:

> It remains for me to pass on to Monseigneur a ring that the Sieur Mattioli gave to Blainvilliers, which he gave to me immediately. I will guard it until it pleases Monseigneur to order me what to do with it . . . I will take the liberty of explaining that I believe that it was as much through fear as for any other reason that he made him this present, as this prisoner had made very insulting remarks to him, and had written some such remarks of a very wicked nature with coaldust on the wall of his room. This had obliged this officer to make him threats of a harsh beating, if he was not more wise and moderate in his remarks in future. When he was put in the tower with the Jacobin, I charged Blainvilliers to tell him, while showing him a bludgeon, that with that one could produce extreme politeness, and that, if he did not mend his ways it would be put to good use. This compliment was made to him, and some days later, when Blainvilliers served him at dinner, he said: 'Monsieur, here is a little ring which I would like to give to you as a present, and which I beg you to accept.' Blainvilliers replied to him that he 'would only take it to give it to me', and that he 'does not receive anything from the prisoners'.

Louvois replied on 2 November: 'You must keep the ring that Sieur Mattioli gave to Sieur de Blainvilliers, to return to him, if ever the King orders that he be set at liberty.'

Another letter followed on 9 June 1681, which seems to refer to the same matter: 'with regard to the effects of Sieur Mattioli which you have, you will only have them carried to Exiles to be able to return them to him, if ever His Majesty orders that he be set at liberty.'

This has been taken to mean that Mattioli was staying with St Mars: it certainly implies that he was going to Exiles.

But there is also evidence, and some useful conjecture,

that Mattioli was not one of the two vital prisoners from the lower tower. The above letters from Louvois entertained a doubt about whether Mattioli would be set at liberty – whereas £6000 had just been spent on a cell for whoever was going to Exiles. Then there is the question of Mattioli's servant. Together with the mad monk, that made three in one cell, but only two men were being transferred. And then there are two letters which strongly imply that Mattioli was left behind at Pignerol. On the first of May 1684, Louvois wrote to St Mars' successor at Pignerol, Governor Villebois:

> I have received your letter of the 14th of last month, from which I perceive the rage of the Sieur Mattioli's servant towards you, and the manner in which you have punished him, which must certainly be approved of, and you ought always to act in the same manner on a like occasion.

A year after Villebois' death in 1692, Barbezieux – now installed at the ministry – wrote to the new governor of Pignerol, La Prade:

> You have merely to burn what remains of the little pieces of the pockets on which Mattioli and his man have written, and which you have found in the lining of their coats, where they had hidden them.

At the same time, over at Exiles, St Mars was asking for a transfer to the scene of Mattioli's crime, the fortress of Casale, by now in French hands at last; hardly a likely request if Mattioli was one of his prisoners.

But the evidence that really seals the matter is provided for us, inadvertently, by St Mars himself. For it was at this point that he made the mistake that spoilt all the careful official 'leaks' which had identified Mattioli as the masked man. The Abbot d'Estrades, the man who had lured Mattioli into the French trap, was still busy with the complicated politics of the North Italian states; and he corresponded with St Mars about what had become of the

Mantuan diplomat who had tried to trick him two years before. The letter in question was not found until centuries later; St Mars' superiors in Paris knew nothing of its existence. But on 25 June 1681, without realising the future significance of what he was doing, St Mars had written to d'Estrades from Pignerol:

> Only yesterday I received my fee as Governor of Exiles ... I shall be keeping my company and two of my lieutenants, and I will be guarding two gaolbirds that I have here, who have no other name than 'the gentlemen of the lower tower'. Mattioli is to stay here with two other prisoners.

The case of Mattioli is not completely sunk: but it is severely scuppered.

The departure for Exiles was a clandestine affair. The governor of the citadel at Pignerol was not told, and St Mars took with him only his most trusted aides – Major Rosarges, Antoine Ru, and William de Formanoir.[2] Perhaps St Mars was moving because some of the regular guards were getting too inquisitive? But whatever the reason, he did not take with him an unscrupulous Italian diplomat called Hercules Anthony Mattioli. There were only two men who could have been in the prisoners' litter that night, two men who were to stay alone with St Mars for the next six years: La Rivière, the valet, and the man named Eustache Dauger.

Notes on Chapter 12

1 *La Prudenza triunfante di Casale*, 1681. *L'Histoire abrégée de l'Europe*, 1687. *Annali d'Italia*, 1749.
2 Blainvilliers had by now been transferred to Metz.

13

The mysterious Eustache

It is frustrating, but hardly surprising, that the most promising candidate so far is the one prisoner whose name – as yet – means nothing. Unlike all the other prisoners, whose previous identities were known, whose crimes were recorded and whose fate can be established, 'Eustache Dauger' remains a mystery. That was a mistake on the part of the king and Louvois. A false name and a plausibly bogus crime would have masked the prisoner forever; but as it is, the obvious secrecy and anonymity heaped upon Eustache cry out for attention. All the evidence will – and must be – presented, before a conclusion can be reached. But from the very first letter, everything about Eustache sounds exactly like 'the man in the iron mask'.

The year is 1669: the date, 19 July, midsummer. Louvois writes to St Mars to tell him to prepare a cell, for a prisoner whose arrest warrant has not yet been written:

Monsieur de St Mars, the King has commanded that I am to have a man named Eustache Dauger sent to Pignerol; it is of the utmost importance to His service that he should be most securely guarded and that he must not be able to give anybody information about himself in any way nor send letters to anyone at all. I am informing you of this in advance so that you can have a cell prepared in which you will put him securely, taking care that the windows of the place in which he is put do

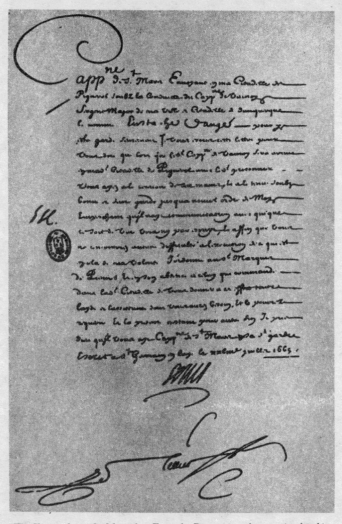

The King informs St Mars that Eustache Dauger is to be committed to his charge, July 1669.

not give on to any places that can be approached by
anyone and that there are multiple doors,[1] for your
sentries not to hear anything. You will yourself once a
day have to take enough food for the day to this wretch
and you must on no account listen for any reason
whatsoever to what he may want to say to you, always
threatening to kill him if he ever opens his mouth to
speak of anything but his necessities.

It was a full nine days later that Captain de Vauroy, the
Sergeant-Major of Dunkirk, was sent orders to arrest
Dauger. The order came from the king himself:

> Captain de Vauroy, as I am dissatisfied with the behav-
> iour of the man named Eustache Dauger and want to
> secure him, I am writing this letter to inform you that as
> soon as you shall see him you are to seize him and to
> conduct him yourself in all safety to the citadel of
> Pignerol, where he is to be guarded by Captain de Saint-
> Mars, to whom I am writing the attached letters so that
> the said prisoner shall be received and guarded there
> without difficulty. After which you are to return from
> there to render an account of that which you shall have
> done in execution of the present order.

King Louis sprayed letters in every direction. He wrote to
St Mars:

> I am sending to my citadel of Pignerol, in the charge of
> Captain de Vauroy, Sergeant-Major of Dunkirk, the man
> named Eustache Dauger. I am writing this letter to
> inform you that when the said Captain de Vauroy arrives
> at my said citadel of Pignerol with the said prisoner, you
> are to receive him and hold him in good and safe custody,
> preventing him from communicating with anyone at all
> by word of mouth or by writing.

And he also wrote to the Marquis de Pienne, town governor
at Pignerol: 'To the Marquis de Pienne, or, in his absence,
to whoever commands the said citadel, to give to the

Seigneurs de Vauroy and de St Mars any aid or assistance that they need or that they may require.'

The whole affair was shrouded in great secrecy. Eustache Dauger was never tried or sentenced; no crime was ever officially attributed to him. The letter to Dunkirk constituted a formal arrest warrant, and as such it should have been entered in the minute of the ministry of war; but in that minute, the name of the prisoner was left blank. This shows that 'Eustache Dauger' must have been a genuine name; for if it was a false name, it would have been entered in order to mislead us. Then there is the register of the king's orders for 1669: all royal orders had to be entered in it. But this order is missing. Obviously, it was important that Eustache Dauger should disappear without trace. If the letter had been entered in the register, it would have required the signature of Jean-Baptiste Colbert,[2] the secretary of state. This suggests that Colbert, who was Louvois' enemy, did not know about Dauger's arrest and might not have approved of it.

The one remaining copy of the arrest order which might arouse suspicion, the one kept at Louvois' office in Paris, was also tampered with, and the name of the prisoner erased. Neither was Captain de Vauroy's superior, the governor of Dunkirk, a former ambassador and a distinguished politician, allowed to know what Vauroy was up to. Louvois simply wrote to him, 'As Monsieur de Vauroy has business which requires him to absent himself, I beg you very humbly to give him leave.'

The cover story was that Vauroy was to arrest any Spanish officers he found pursuing deserters from the Spanish Netherlands. No similar order was given to anyone else in the area; but it was a reasonably convincing tale to tell the troops about the man they were arresting. In fact, this order excusing Vauroy and his men was written on the same day as the first letter to St Mars, but well before the formal warrant naming Eustache Dauger arrived in Dunkirk. So it could be that Eustache was already being hunted, maybe that he had already been arrested and was on his way to interrogation, by the time any formal permission to arrest him reached Captain de Vauroy.

The letters to St Mars about Dauger's arrest are awash with clues. The fact that Dauger's cell was ready in advance, and that only the sergeant-major from Dunkirk was alerted to arrest him, shows that not only was Dauger expected, but that they knew when and where to expect him too. Vauroy was told to arrest 'the man named Eustache Dauger' – in other words, he already knew who he was and what he looked like. Vauroy's expenses claim for the trip shows that he and his men visited both Dunkirk and Calais before heading south for Pignerol. The fact that Dauger was arrested in a Northern French port probably means that he was trying to flee the country. Dunkirk and Calais were the principal departure points out of Northern France, for the Belgian border was shut. So we have another piece of information; Dauger almost certainly knew he was being hunted, and was trying to get away. But somebody had tipped off the authorities.

Certainly, Eustache fits the general requirements for being the masked man. He was presumably French, for he had a French name and the guards were expected to understand him if he spoke. He was arrested in the right year, 1669. He does not contradict Louis xv's proviso that no theories advanced before the 1720s were correct. As the longest-serving of St Mars' prisoners by March 1680, he fits the description 'ancient prisoner'. And the incredible security surrounding him tallies with that provided for the masked man. But a curious reference, on the end of Louvois' initial letter to St Mars, has led variously to Dauger being dismissed as nothing more than an unimportant servant, or to his being linked with Martin the Valet:

> I shall instruct Sieur Poupart to set to work without delay on whatever you may require, and to make for you the furniture which will be necessary for the man that is being sent to you, bearing in mind that, as he is only a valet he does not require anything special; and I will

reimburse you such expense as you desire for the furniture and for his food.

'A valet that does not require anything special' would seem
to stop us in our tracks. Could this really be the man in the
mask? But the letter needs more investigation – who was
this 'Sieur Poupart'?

Poupart was, in fact, the minister in charge of fortifications. The minister himself made a six-week journey across
the mountains, to supervise personally the equipping of the
new cell. There were already five empty cells at Pignerol,
thought strong enough to hold the likes of Nicolas Fouquet;
there was already plenty of prison furniture; and there was
already a budget for food and other necessities. But this
prisoner had his own special cell, which took six months to
build, and his own budget. Why was the minister of
fortifications travelling all that way just for one man? Who
could such a prisoner be?

The letter is more or less a contradiction in terms, unless
it holds an obscure meaning. For if Eustache was really
'only a valet' he wouldn't have lasted long. But there are
possible explanations. Most convincingly, Major R. Ansell
Wells has pointed out that the term 'valet' is common
French slang for a toady or crawler, as any dictionary will
testify. Louvois, who disliked his expensive prisoner, may
simply have been insulting him, leading St Mars to grasp
the wrong end of the stick. Alternatively, it was also a
common trick to impute a lowly status to important prisoners, so as not to arouse suspicion. Calling Eustache
Dauger a 'valet' was certainly a brilliant excuse as to why
he need not be provided with one. The whole business led
to much confusion later on.

Of course, it is not impossible that the prisoner was a
gentleman who had fallen on hard times and had become a
'gentleman's gentleman' in order to make ends meet, a
comedown that Louvois would no doubt have relished. If
Dauger was a valet, it is certain that he was not an ordinary
one. St Mars himself never seemed entirely sure of his

prisoner's true status; but he was clearly aware, at least, of his prisoner's enormous importance. The security measures were ferocious.

> Monsieur de Vauroy has given the man named Eustache d'Auger into my hands. As soon as I had put him in a very secure place, while waiting for the cell I am having prepared for him to be completed, I told him, in the presence of Monsieur de Vauroy, that if he should speak to me or to anyone else, of anything other than his necessities, I would run my sword through his stomach. On my life, I shall not fail to observe very punctiliously your commands ... there is nothing truer than that I have never spoken of this prisoner to anyone; and as proof of this, many people here believe that he is a Marshal of France, and others say 'a President'.

The legend had begun.

Other letters follow on, each providing us with further pieces of information. Louvois informs us that Dauger is a Catholic, another prerequisite for any candidate who would be the man in the mask:

> You can give a prayer book to your new prisoner, and if he asks you for any other [prayer book], give it him also. You can let him hear on Sundays and Feast days the Mass that is said for Monsieur Fouquet without however being in the same place, and you will see that he is so well guarded during that time, that he cannot escape or speak to anyone: you can even let him have confession three or four times a year, if he wants it.

When Dauger is ill, St Mars is to have a free hand:

> When the prisoner is ill, you can have him treated and doctored according to his needs without waiting for an order for that, only giving me an account of what has occurred.

St Mars is instructed to try to make all his prisoners and their valets speak, except Dauger. He is to report the slightest things they say, but he is to prevent Dauger from saying the slightest thing. And Dauger, like the masked man of the Bastille, remains placid:

> As for the prisoner of the tower that Monsieur de Vauroy brought to me, he says nothing. He lives contentedly, like a man utterly resigned to the wishes of God and King.

Here, at last, is one reference we have been looking for – 'the prisoner of the tower that Monsieur de Vauroy brought to me'; showing that Eustache, too, fits the nickname 'La Tour', the man of the tower.

In April 1670 comes a letter that has already been referred to. St Mars tells Louvois that:

> There are people who are sometimes so curious in asking me for information of my prisoner, or the reason why I take so many precautions for his security, that I am obliged to tell them tall stories.

The words 'my prisoner' can only be a reference to Dauger. At this time only he and Fouquet were at Pignerol, and Fouquet's imprisonment was no secret: in fact, a few years before, when an explosion in the powder magazine had put the cells at Pignerol out of action, Fouquet had been 'billeted' in the town. He was trusted to behave himself in public. Dauger, on the other hand, was not even allowed to speak to his guards. All St Mars' prisoners were referred to by name, except Dauger; he usually became 'my prisoner' or 'the prisoner from Dunkirk'.

Despite his generally good behaviour, Fouquet was naturally overcome by curiosity about the new arrival. Louvois, who had spies everywhere, was not slow to notice it. And he was not best pleased with St Mars:

> I have been advised that Monsieur Honneste, one of Monsieur Fouquet's valets, has spoken to the prisoner who was brought to you by the Major of Dunkirk, and has asked him, among other things, if he had nothing of

consequence to say to him, to which he replied he should be left in peace: he behaved in this way, believing probably that this was someone from you who was questioning him to test him, and see if he would say something; from this you can well see you have not taken enough precautions to prevent him from having any communications at all; and, as it is very important for His Majesty's service, that he should have none, I bid you to inspect carefully the inside and outside of the place where he is imprisoned and to put it in a state that the prisoner cannot see or be seen by anyone, and cannot speak to anyone, nor hear those who might wish to tell him something.

In fairness to St Mars, it must be said that Dauger's new cell, the triple-doored affair, was not completed until May 1670; whereas Honneste's enquiries were made several weeks before. But it was not long afterwards that Louvois himself journeyed to Pignerol to check the security precautions. He took with him a building expert, Vauban, to add new fortifications and security measures.

For the minister of war to make a trip like this was unheard of – four hundred miles to Briançon, then some seventy miles on rough, unsurfaced mountain roads to Pignerol, about a week in each direction – just for one man. He certainly wasn't coming to check the security arrangements for Fouquet, who had been allowed to board in the town. And he certainly didn't want his visit to arouse suspicion locally; instead of staying with the local prefect, as would be expected of him, he stayed discreetly with the Count of Falcombel, an old and trusted friend. Yet the news must have leaked out, for Voltaire knew of the visit, even if he got the location mixed up. He wrote: 'The Marquis de Louvois went to see him . . . and spoke to him, without sitting down, in a manner which showed great respect.'

The king and Louvois acted quickly upon the minister's return to Paris. Louvois informed his representative at

Pignerol, Loyauté, that the king had decided to remove both the town governor and the governor of the citadel; only St Mars was to keep his job. And remove them Louis did – along with an entire regiment, the Lyonnais, which was moved to the interior at his personal command. Historians suggest that the Lyonnais were transferred in order to attack Casale, which may be so, but the fact remains that no such order was given until ten years later, after the Mattioli affair.

It is at about this time that our third candidate, the valet La Rivière, is introduced. A year previously, one of Fouquet's valets, Laforêt, had been discovered plotting Fouquet's escape. He was tried, sentenced to death and executed by St Mars on the spot.[3] Honneste, who had helped, was eventually removed from Pignerol, leaving Fouquet with two valets: Champagne, who was to die four years later, ánd La Rivière, who was to leave Pignerol with Dauger. It was the illness and death of Champagne that led – indirectly – to the curious pairing of Eustache and La Rivière on the coach to Exiles. It is these circumstances which must now be investigated, to show that these were indeed the two 'gentlemen of the lower tower'.

By 1670, illness was becoming a problem at Pignerol. St Mars wrote to Louvois, 'Monsieur Fouquet has a little fever which does not inconvenience him a great deal, but one of his valets is very ill, as also is the prisoner who was sent to me.' Frequently, there were not the valets available to serve Fouquet, or the Count of Lauzun when he arrived in 1671. So St Mars had a bright idea: why not put the 'valet' from Dunkirk to good use?

> It is so difficult to find valets here who are willing to shut themselves up with my prisoners that I would take the liberty of proposing one to you: that prisoner who is in the tower and whom you sent to me by Monsieur the Major of Dunkirk, would be, it seems to me, a good valet. I do not think he would say to Monsieur Lauzun

where he comes from after I had forbidden him to do so;
I am sure that he would not give him any information,
nor ask me to let him go out all the time, as all the others
do . . . I would achieve the impossible if I were to find
anyone here to give [Lauzun]. None of my valets would
enter there for a million francs. They have seen that
those whom I have placed with Monsieur Fouquet never
come out.

St Mars promised not to look for a new valet for Lauzun
until he received a reply concerning 'the man in the
tower'.

Not surprisingly, the answer was no. There was absolutely no question of Dauger meeting the Count. But this is
an interesting letter. Quite apart from confirming that
Dauger had become known as 'l'homme de la tour', the
man in the tower, it shows that St Mars obviously saw
Dauger as a quiet, inoffensive prisoner, who might make a
good valet. He was prepared to vouch for Dauger's discretion, and had probably taken pity on him. At any rate,
his request seems to have sown a seed in the minds of
Louvois and the king.

On 5 February 1674 Fouquet wrote to his wife to say
that the valet Champagne had died, and that his other
valet La Rivière was constantly ill. It appears that La
Rivière suffered from dropsy, an unpleasant form of water-
retention. Finding a replacement would obviously be difficult, so on 30 January 1675 Louvois and the king finally
decided to implement St Mars' suggestion, but with a
proviso:

His Majesty approves that you give, as valet to Monsieur
Fouquet, the prisoner whom Monsieur de Vauroy
brought to you; but whatever happens, you must refrain
from putting him with Monsieur de Lauzun, or with
anyone else other than Monsieur Fouquet.

I am sir, your obedient servant,
de Louvois.

That is to say, that you can give the said prisoner to Monsieur Fouquet, if his valet should fail him and not otherwise.

Soon afterwards, he wrote again to make doubly sure:

If you can find a valet who is suitable to serve Monsieur de Lauzun, you may give him to him; but you must not for any conceivable reason give him the prisoner that Monsieur de Vauroy brought to you, who must only serve, in case of necessity, Monsieur Fouquet, as I have informed you.

We have here something of a predicament; but perhaps it is one that can be solved. Eustache Dauger is allowed to act as a valet, but he is a valet who is visited by ministers, who has thousands spent upon him and has special cells built to house him. Which seems to imply that he is not a valet. He may speak to Fouquet, and only Fouquet, whereas he is threatened with instant death if he speaks to his guards. He may on no account speak to the Count of Lauzun, or anyone else for that matter, but especially not to Lauzun.

It is a difficult problem. To get behind it we must try to understand something of Nicolas Fouquet's situation. True, he was a prisoner; but he was treated well, he was allowed to go for walks in the citadel, and above all, he was *trusted*. Behaving well, and repaying the king's trust, was the only way back for Fouquet; it was not uncommon for politicians to be gaoled and then to return to positions of eminence. No real taint was involved. And so, while imprisoned at Pignerol, Fouquet was very much the king's man.

In his day – before 1661 – he had known everything of consequence in France. So it is likely that whatever Eustache Dauger knew, it had happened before 1661, that Fouquet already knew what it was, and that he could be trusted with it. Thus they were allowed to talk to each other. They may even have met, before Fouquet was arrested. At least this goes some way to explaining the remark of Chamillart, the minister of war after Barbezieux, connecting the two. Whoever Eustache Dauger was, and whatever he had done in 1669, it seems that the Count of Lauzun was somehow involved as well, for it was especially forbidden for him to encounter Eustache. But valets who know state secrets do not hobnob with ministers and counts in expensive rooms; they are quickly and quietly done away with. Fouquet's first valet had apparently been done away with in the 1660s, simply for helping his master make pen and ink from chicken bones and soot. So was Dauger a valet or not?

It seems likely that Louvois and the king finally agreed to St Mars' idea in order to give Dauger some company, for prisoners in solitary confinement frequently went mad. Dauger did not sleep in Fouquet's room like a valet, but kept his own cell. If Fouquet knew who he was, as seems likely, he would know whether or not he was a real valet and would treat him accordingly. Even if his new companion had ever tried his hand at being a valet, there is one piece of evidence that suggests Fouquet would have recognised Dauger for a gentleman rather than a servant. That is the fact that only Eustache, Fouquet and Lauzun – the others a minister and a count – were never beaten, intimidated or maltreated. St Mars was ordered and expected to give them good treatment. Once, before his arrest, the Count of Lauzun had been insolent to the king, who had been tempted to strike him: instead, he dashed his cane at the window 'so as not to have to beat a gentleman'. It was an easy matter to decapitate a gentleman but unthinkable to lay a hand on one. The qualification was certainly high – such as Mattioli, an Italian minister, did not pass muster. Only a French minister, a count, and our 'valet' were considered gentleman enough to avoid being touched.

We shall return fully to Messrs Fouquet and Lauzun in due course. But for the time being, the new arrangements seemed suitable to all concerned. There was, however, one fly in the ointment – La Rivière. Dauger was only supposed to speak to Fouquet when La Rivière 'failed' his master;

but had La Rivière discovered anything by mistake? Towards Christmas-time 1678, Louvois sent a special packet to St Mars:

> I enclose a letter for Monsieur Fouquet: it is the intention of the King that you give it to him sealed, as you receive it; that you take into his chamber ink, paper, a seal and some wax, and that you leave it there so that he can reply at his leisure, and that you address the letter that he gives you to me, with seal unbroken . . .

St Mars was to see nothing. The letter he passed on to Fouquet offered a straightforward swap:

> Monsieur, it is with much pleasure that I conform to the command that it has pleased the King to give me, to advise you that His Majesty is disposed to grant in a little while very considerable alleviations to your imprisonment; but, as he desires first of all to be informed whether the man called Eustache, who was given to you as your valet, has not spoken before the other valet who served you of that which he was doing before being at Pignerol[4]: His Majesty has commanded me to ask you this and to tell you that he expects that, without any prior consideration, you will report to me the truth regarding the above, so that he can take the measures that he will consider most appropriate about what he will learn from you that the said Eustache may have said about his past life to his comrade. The intention of His Majesty is that you should reply to this letter, in your own room, without conveying anything of what it contains to Monsieur de Saint-Mars, to whom I am writing that the King desires he should give you some paper.

This makes it crystal clear that Fouquet was fully aware of Eustache's secret. It also explains why La Rivière joined Eustache in the lower tower after Fouquet's death, condemned by his master. In 1669, before meeting Dauger, La Rivière was being considered for release. Louvois had written to St Mars, 'His Majesty leaves it to you to act as you please with respect to La Rivière, that is to say, to leave him with Monsieur Fouquet or to remove him.' Yet there was no question of his ever being released now. Fouquet, ever loyal to his king, had sold his valet's freedom. Fouquet certainly got his promised improvements; including visits from his family, from local prostitutes, and even well-guarded talks with Lauzun. But Eustache had to be kept well hidden, as Louvois told St Mars in January 1679:

> Each time that Monsieur Fouquet goes down into Monsieur de Lauzun's chamber, or that Monsieur de Lauzun goes up into Monsieur Fouquet's chamber, or some other stranger, Monsieur de Saint-Mars will take care to withdraw the man called Eustache and will not put him back into the chamber of Monsieur Fouquet, until there is nobody else left but he and his old valet. He will do the same when Monsieur Fouquet goes for a walk in the citadel, making the said Eustache remain in Monsieur Fouquet's room.

The king never ceased to fret about Dauger. 'See that he speaks to no-one in private', came the letters, 'send me news of Eustache Dauger's health.'

But soon afterwards, on 8 April 1680, came a letter with immense significance for Eustache Dauger and La Rivière. For Fouquet had died after a sudden illness, and their relatively convenient lifestyle was about to take a change for the worse. Louvois told St Mars:

> The King has learnt, from the letter you wrote to me on the 23rd of last month, of the death of Monsieur Fouquet, and the opinion you have formed that Monsieur de Lauzun knows most of the important matters with which Monsieur Fouquet was acquainted, and that the man named La Rivière is not ignorant of them either . . . you should persuade Monsieur de Lauzun that the man named Eustache d'Augers, and the said La Rivière, have been set at liberty, and that you should tell the same to all those who may ask you for news of them; that

Louvois' letter of 10 July 1680, distinguishing Mattioli from the 'prisoners of the lower tower'.

nevertheless you should shut them both in a room where you can assure His Majesty they will have no communication with anyone at all, neither by word of mouth, nor by writing, and that Monsieur de Lauzun* will not be able to perceive that they are shut in it . . . I am adding these words to tell you that you must not enter into any discourse or confidence with Monsieur de Lauzun regarding what he may have learned from Monsieur Fouquet.

Lauzun was not to know it, but La Rivière – who by rights should have been released – was to join Eustache in the lower tower, a prisoner in his own right. Usually, a valet who had done something wrong or who knew too much was simply killed – like Laforêt. But La Rivière was spared – why? One can only presume that he was to provide company for the masked man.

Henceforth the pair became 'the prisoners of the lower tower'. A letter of July 1680 records that 'it will suffice to confess the prisoners of the lower tower once a year. With regard to the Sieur de Lestang . . .' The letter continues with a fresh set of instructions for a different man – Mattioli. As St Mars let slip in his letter to the Abbot of Estrades, Mattioli was staying at Pignerol, while his 'two gaolbirds' from the lower tower went with him to Exiles in 1681. In fact, St Mars even wanted to bring Dauger's triple doors from Pignerol to Exiles, to keep him extra safe. There was no need, said Louvois. New doors would be made, as part of an even bigger, more secure cell.

In keeping with instructions never to refer to these gentlemen by their real names again, the words 'Dauger' and 'La Rivière' disappeared almost completely from the correspondence. Even tell-tale descriptions like 'the prisoner from Dunkirk' or 'Monsieur Vauroy's prisoner' are no longer used. In their place appears one 'masked man'. Mattioli, languishing at Pignerol under his own name, waits to rejoin them. Which of these prisoners went to his death at the Bastille? The correspondence must now be

followed to its end on the Isles of Sainte-Marguerite to find
the final proof.

Notes on Chapter 13

1 In fact there were three doors, as a later letter mentioned.
2 Brother of the French ambassador to London, whom we have
already encountered in the case of the Abbot Pregnani.
3 Laforêt was hanged before Fouquet's very eyes.
4 Interestingly, the phrase 'that which he was doing before being
at Pignerol' is a correction. The original text read, 'that which he
had *seen* before being at Pignerol'.

14

Exiles to the islands

So that no-one can see the prisoners, they will not leave their room to hear Mass; and in order to keep them in greater security, one of my lieutenants will sleep above them, and there will be two sentinels day and night, who will watch all round the tower, without they or the prisoners being able to see or speak to one another, or even to hear anything; they will be soldiers of my company, who will always be placed on guard. There is only a confessor who worries me a little; but if Monseigneur judges it correct I will give them the curate of Exiles instead, who is a good man, and very old, whom I will forbid, on the part of His Majesty, to enquire who these prisoners are, or their names, or what they have been, or ever to speak to them in any way, or to receive from them by word of mouth, or by writing, any communications or notes.

Such was life for the two prisoners at the fortress of Exiles. According to St Mars, they were 'extremely quiet'. But his Majesty was not satisfied.

As it is important to prevent the prisoners who are at Exiles, who were named 'of the lower tower' at Pignerol, from having any communications, the King has ordered me to command you to have them so strictly guarded and to take such precautions that you will be able to reply to His Majesty that they will speak to no-one, not only from outside, but even of the garrison of Exiles; I bid you report to me from time to time what is happening to them.

St Mars reported again.

These prisoners can hear the people speak who pass along the road which is at the bottom of the tower where they are; but they, if they wish it, could not make themselves heard; they can see the persons who are on the hill which is before their windows, but they cannot themselves be seen on account of the bars which are in front of their rooms. I have two sentinels of my company, night and day, on each side of the tower, at a reasonable distance, who can see the windows of the prisoners obliquely. They are ordered not to listen should anyone speak to them, and that they [the prisoners] do not cry out from their windows; and to make the passers-by who stop on the road or on the side of the hill walk on. My room, being joined to the tower, which has no other view except towards the path, means that I hear and see everything, even my two sentinels, who are by this means always kept alert.

As for the inside of the tower, I have divided it in such a manner that the priest who says Mass to them cannot see them, on account of the barrier I have made, which covers their double doors. The servants, who bring their food, put that which is necessary for the prisoners upon a table on the outside, and my lieutenant takes it and carries it in. No-one speaks to them except myself, my officer, Monseigneur Vigneron (the old curate) and a doctor from Pragelas, six leagues from here, and only in my presence.

Six prisoners had entered the gates of Pignerol and were never to escape the clutches of St Mars. One – Fouquet – was dead. One – the mad monk – was to die at Pignerol when St Mars had gone. Dubreuil the spy and Mattioli the diplomat had remained there, ready to rejoin their gaoler later. But these two men – Eustache Dauger and La Rivière the valet – were to stay with St Mars wherever he went. And one of these two was almost certainly the masked man. To ensure the secrecy of their transfer to Exiles, the ubiquitous Marshal Castinat and a brother officer had temporarily taken their place at Pignerol, to keep the number of prisoners at six until Dauger and La Rivière were long gone.

The prison they found themselves in, the fortress of Exiles, consisted of two towers overlooking a mountain pass, where fifty handpicked men watched them day and night. But still the security measures did not satisfy His Majesty. Confession, which had originally been allowed a handful of times a year at Pignerol, then once a year, was reduced even further: 'I think that you know that the prisoners who are under your guard must only be confessed following an order from the King, or in imminent peril of death; you will kindly observe the above.' Imprisonment, for the two prisoners of Exiles, was getting even more rigorous.

Only one of the two men lived long enough to go with St Mars to the islands of Sainte-Marguerite – only one became the masked man. Indications that one was indeed in 'imminent peril of death' were present from 1681, the first year of captivity in their new prison. St Mars complained: 'As there is always one of my two prisoners ill, they give me as much occupation as I have ever had with [any of] those I have guarded before.'

A clue, perhaps, slipped out in April 1684. Louvois commanded: 'Report to me what you know of the birth of the man named La Rivière and of the circumstances by which he was placed at the service of the late Monsieur Fouquet.' Was La Rivière the dying prisoner? Another letter, in June 1685, would seem to suggest this: 'You can report to me in detail what the intention is of that one of your prisoners who wants to make his will, and, if you mark on the outside of your letter that it is to be handed to me personally, no-one will open it.'

The idea that Dauger – who had been spirited away from the world without trial or record – would be allowed to make a will, is extremely unlikely. La Rivière, on the other hand, was known by his relatives to be serving in prison, and had wages accumulated but unable to spend which he could pass on to them in death. It was La Rivière who suffered from dropsy: an important clue, in the light of the letters which hurried to and fro between Paris and Exiles throughout 1686:

> You should have named to me which of your prisoners it is that has become dropsical . . . It is right to have that one of your two prisoners who had become dropsical confessed, when you perceive the signs of an approaching death. Until then neither he nor his companion must have any communication [with anyone].

On 5 January 1687 St Mars announced the death of the prisoner who had suffered from dropsy. One can only presume that it was La Rivière. After all, it was Eustache, not La Rivière, who had been arrested in 1669, who must not be recognised. La Rivière was only ever an ordinary valet, who had stumbled unwittingly upon a great secret. Nobody would recognise a valet. Remember Father Papon's story, of the very important prisoner, whose man-servant had just died? Eustache Dauger, the original owner of the secret, had lived on to become the masked man; his companion it was that had died.

The letter announcing La Rivière's death crossed paths on its way to Paris with one coming in the opposite direction addressed to St Mars:

> As the King has kindly seen fit to grant you the Governorship of the Isles of Sainte-Marguerite, I can inform you with pleasure thereof, in order that you can hold yourself in readiness to go to the said islands as soon as you receive orders to do so from His Majesty, whose intention is that as soon as you have received your commission, you should go and inspect the said Isles, to

see what has to be done to prepare a place suitable for guarding securely the prisoners who are in your charge, of which you will send me a plan and memorandum, so that I can obtain His Majesty's opinion for working at it. Meanwhile, you will return to Exiles, to await the necessary orders of His Majesty to take them there, as well as your company. I think that it is unnecessary for me to advise you to take such measures that, during the time you will require to go to the Isles of Sainte-Marguerite and return, the said prisoners will be guarded in a manner that no mishap can occur and that they will have no communication with anyone.

The masked man was coming to Sainte-Marguerite.

Today, the remains of the famous prison are still perched above the rocks of Sainte-Marguerite. The masked man's cell, specially built by St Mars, also remains. It is tall and light, with large windows and a vaulted roof; a comfortable prison. But it also had triple studded doors and four rows of thick crossbars on the windows: St Mars told Louvois that there was no stronger or safer accommodation in Europe. 'I am taking the liberty, my Lord,' he wrote, 'to inform you in detail of the excellence of this spot for when you have prisoners you want to place in complete security with reasonable liberty.' There were other prisoners at Sainte-Marguerite, Protestant prisoners, maintained securely on a few sous each day, in ordinary cells. But that wasn't good enough for Dauger. His one room alone cost over £5000 to build. Thousands were spent on his upkeep. St Mars even had to keep the details of his expenditure on the prisoner obscure. 'I am not putting it in detail', he told Louvois, 'so that nobody through whose hands it passes can discover anything other than what they can guess.' Even the civil servants at the ministry were to be kept ignorant of the secret royal guest.

Two remarks seem to contradict this picture of an important, well-fed prisoner. In December 1681 Louvois instructed St Mars to buy new clothes for his prisoners,

then added, 'but the clothes of fellows like these must last
for three or four years'. And six years later, after arriving
at Sainte-Marguerite, St Mars sold his prisoner's old
furniture. He wrote: 'My prisoner's bed was so old and
worn out, also everything which he used, table linen as well
as furniture, that they were scarcely worth bringing here,
and they only fetched thirteen crowns.'

Once again, Louvois appears to have contradicted himself. He says that the prisoners' clothes should last a few
years, yet in June of the same year he was paying St Mars
£4,380 for their annual upkeep. As for selling the furniture,
a price of thirteen crowns – about £40, or £400 in today's
money – was no mean sum, when one bears in mind how
little was spent on other prisoners; here was an inmate that
used table linen. But nonetheless the furniture of such a
wealthy prisoner should not have become 'old and worn
out'. There seems to have been some conflict and confusion
among the authorities themselves as to just how well the
'ancient prisoner' should be treated. Perhaps St Mars was
raking off a substantial proportion of his prisoner's wealth
– not an uncommon practice for a seventeenth-century
gaoler. The only indisputable factor was Louvois' need for
even more stringent security measures.

Again, one is tempted to wonder about the alternative
candidate – Mattioli. In March 1694, as the forces of the
Duke of Savoy threatened Pignerol, the prisoners there
were evacuated, and sent to join St Mars at the Isles of
Sainte-Marguerite. A special, secure cell – another one –
was prepared to receive Mattioli. Louvois had met his
curious death in 1691 and his son and successor Barbezieux
told St Mars to expect the new arrivals. He wrote: 'Since
you know that they are of more consequence, at least one,
than those who are at present in the Isles, you must, in
preference to those others, put them in the more secure
cells.' Does this mean that Mattioli – previously 'not
important' enough to go to Exiles – was now *more* important
than Eustache Dauger? That when the two were in the
same prison, Mattioli was to get the star treatment? Did

the phrase 'your ancient prisoner' perhaps really mean 'your former prisoner' and refer to Mattioli? So it would seem on the face of it.

In fact, the evidence against this and in favour of Dauger is overwhelming. In the first place, it is worth remembering that St Mars had in his charge on Sainte-Marguerite a gaggle of unruly Protestant ministers; it was they whose security was less important. Eustache Dauger never moved from his three-doored, four-barred, five-star cell, neither for Mattioli nor for anybody else. The phrase 'at least one' can also be questioned. For the original French phrase, 'au moins qu'un', is very similar to the French phrase for 'except one', 'à moins qu'un'. So similar, in fact, that contemporary instances exist of the one being used to signify the other. So this letter could mean that the new prisoners were more important, except for one man.

Less speculative is the vital contrast between the journeys of Dauger and Mattioli to their new home. The journey of Eustache Dauger from Exiles to the Isles of Sainte-Marguerite was shrouded in secrecy; so strict were the security precautions, in fact, that the prisoner almost died. The idea came from St Mars:

> I will give such good orders for the guarding of my prisoner, that I can answer to you, Monseigneur, for his entire security, and even for the conversation that I have always prevented his having with my lieutenant. If I take him to the Isles, I think that the most secure transport will be a chair covered with waxed cloth, in which there would enter a sufficiency of air, without it being possible for anyone to see or speak to him during the journey, not even the soldiers whom I shall select to be near the chair, which will be less embarrassing than a litter, which can often break down.

It was not tremendously successful. St Mars' report read:

> I arrived here on the 30 of last month. I stayed only twelve days on the road, because my prisoner was ill: he

said that he had not as much air as he wished. I can assure you, sir, that nobody saw him at all, and that the way in which I guarded and conducted him during the whole journey caused each passer-by to try and guess who my prisoner was ... I have given to eight porters who brought the chair from Turin and my prisoner as far as here, including the cost of the said chair, £203, which I have distributed.

These expensive Italian porters are an important clue. There were forty-five unemployed soldiers escorting the carriage: but eight porters had to be hired from Turin at great cost to carry the prisoner. The reason is obvious. The Turinese porters would speak no French, and the masked man in his sedan chair no Italian. It proves, at least, that the Italian Mattioli was not the man receiving such treatment. When Mattioli did make his journey from Pignerol, in the March snows of 1694, it was altogether a different story. The prisoners had to walk the 100 kilometres themselves in freezing temperatures, a six-day journey across the Alps. St Mars did not bother to accompany them, but stayed on the island with Dauger. So bad was the journey, in fact, that one of the prisoners died of exhaustion only ten days later. And here is our last but most important clue.

We know from the orders of the escort Captain, de Maisonel, that he marched four prisoners across the Alps in a series of seventeenth-century chain gangs: Mattioli, his valet, Dubreuil the spy, and a new man named de Herse. The mad monk had died only two months before. We also know that both Mattioli and his valet were ill. In the light of these facts, the letter written by Barbezieux to St Mars on 10 May 1694, is particularly important:

> You must, as you propose, have the valet of the prisoner who died put in the vaulted prison,[1] taking care to have him as carefully guarded as the others.

Mattioli must have been the prisoner that died. He was the only one of the three on the transport party with a valet, and he had been ill. Neither Dauger nor any of the Protestant ministers had valets in 1694. We have seen all along how Mattioli was undoubtedly an important prisoner, to be treated securely: the fact that his valet was not going to be released confirms that. But the death of a prisoner who must surely have been Mattioli in 1694 proves that he was not the man in the mask.

It is possible to corroborate the story of Mattioli's death by turning to the evidence of Claude Souchon, whose father was a cadet in St Mars' company. Questioned about the man in the iron mask, Souchon insisted the masked man was an envoy of the Count of Turin, and that he had died at Sainte-Marguerite nine years after his arrest in 1685: he had had a valet who had also died there. Mattioli fits this jumbled description quite well. Although he was actually arrested in 1679, the mistaken date of 1685 was commonly thought to be correct at the time of Souchon's testimony – so Mattioli's death nine years later in 1694 fits correctly. Furthermore, his valet did indeed die at Sainte-Marguerite after him – in 1701. Claude Souchon was mistaken in thinking that he had described the iron mask; but his memories have proved equally important in a way that he could never have realised, by ruling out the man he sought to identify. While his father remembered well the death of the quarrelsome Italian diplomat, it is possible that he never even noticed what became of the quiet recluse whose meals were served by officers, or by the governor himself.

Henceforth, there was only one ancient prisoner, who preoccupied the authorities continuously, but who went uncomplaining to the Bastille in 1698. There was only one candidate who fitted the ancient prisoner's description – Eustache Dauger. When Barbezieux had inherited the war ministry from his father in 1691, he had written: 'When you have something to report to me about the prisoner that you have had in your custody for twenty years, I bid you to take the same precautions as you used when you gave news of him to Monsieur de Louvois.' As we now know, it is a reference that could only apply to Dauger. Indeed, if

Eustache was not the masked man, then the mystery of
Eustache's identity is a greater mystery than that of the
masked man itself.

Life at Sainte-Marguerite continued in the same vein as
at Pignerol and Exiles. Even when St Mars was away or ill,
precautions were not relaxed for the 'ancient prisoner'. His
food was served by two lieutenants, probably Rosarges and
Lamotte-Guérin:

> The first of my lieutenants . . . opens the three doors and
> enters the chamber of the prisoner, who politely hands
> him the plates and dishes, which he has put one on top
> of the other, to give them into the hands of the lieutenant,
> who has only to go through two doors to hand them to
> one of my sergeants, who takes them and places them on
> a table two steps away, where is the second lieutenant,
> who examines everything that enters and leaves the
> prison, and sees that there is nothing written on the
> plate: and after they have given him the necessary
> utensil, they examine his bed inside and out, and then
> the gratings of the windows, and all around it, and very
> often the man himself: after having asked him very
> politely if he needs anything else, they lock the doors.

Security was still fierce. Just like Dauger at Pignerol, the
ancient prisoner had his three doors. But the same guards
that were sent to flog the other prisoners were told to ask
Dauger very politely if there was anything else he needed.

On the first of March, 1698, St Mars was appointed to
the governorship of the Bastille in Paris. It was the top of
his profession. From that point, the letters stop: five years
later, the ancient prisoner was dead, and five years after
that, so was St Mars. But two remaining letters from the
years leading up to 1698 provide vital clues. Both were
written by Barbezieux to St Mars, the first in November
1697:

> You have no other duty to observe with regard to all
> those who are entrusted to your custody than to continue

Louis XIV (picture by Rigaud at the Louvre) and insert of Louis de Cavoye

Jean-Baptiste Colbert (picture by Nanteuil)

The Count of Lauzun

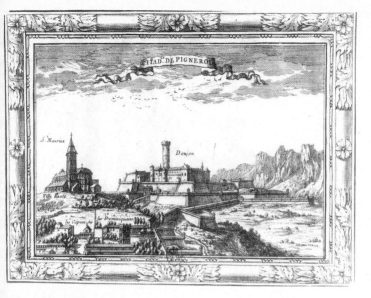

The prison at Pignerol

The Bastille

1 Bastille   2 Cemetery of St Paul   3 Rue Vivienne

Palais Royal   5 Rue Sourdière   6 Rue de Bourbon   7 Charity Hospital

The prison on the Île Sainte-Marguerite

to see to their security without explaining to anyone whatsoever what your ancient prisoner has done.

But St Mars wasn't supposed to know what his ancient prisoner had done. Even if the old gaoler had discovered the masked man's secret, he was sufficiently careful to stay silent about it, in case he too was shut up for life. This could be a reference to the story of the writing on the silver plate found by the illiterate peasant. Or, alternatively, it could mean that Eustache had committed another crime, inside his prison. This is an option that will require further investigation.

On 15 June 1698 St Mars was ordered to move, and 'to take with you in all security your ancient prisoner'. His companion of twenty-nine years was to stay with him. Our final letter, written on 19 July, deals with that move. Barbezieux wrote:

> The King approves that you should leave the Isles of Sainte-Marguerite to go to the Bastille with your ancient prisoner, taking all precautions to prevent his being seen or recognised by anyone. You can write in advance to His Majesty's Lieutenant at that fortress to have a chamber ready so as to be able to place your prisoner in it on your arrival.

It was important that the masked prisoner should not be seen *or recognised* en route. But after almost thirty years, who would recognise him? In an age without mass communications only one face was so recognisable – a royal face. Or perhaps a face that resembled a royal face?

If the masked man really had such a recognisable face, then St Mars must have been capable of a few shrewd guesses as to his identity. But the rewards for keeping his guesses to himself were immense: £40,000 a year, a huge salary even by today's standards. St Mars was now an incredibly rich man, being unable to spend his fortune: only twice, in 1682 and 1685, was he allowed to take a few day's leave on his own business. Promotion to the Bastille, for such an obscure little man, was unheard of. Even more unusual was the fact that he brought his own staff with him, down to the humblest door-opener. But St Mars knew and trusted Antoine Ru; he was not the man to spill his secrets in a Parisian tavern. And so, one morning late in August 1698, St Mars and his little family of gaolers set out for the capital, with a small escort of soldiers and their ever-present prisoner, in his sealed litter. As we know, they stopped en route at St Mars' chateau of Palteau, where his pistols, his locked doors and his mysterious masked charge startled the peasants. Then the procession set out again, to disappear from history for ever.

Eustache Dauger, the tranquil, silent prisoner from Dunkirk, who looked like somebody so important that he had to be covered up, who knew something so important that he had to be silenced, who had done something so terrible that he had to be punished, was the man in the mask. Had anyone else been the masked man, such as Mattioli the diplomat, or the mad monk, the investigation would be over. But the three basic questions that comprise this mystery – his identity, his secret and his crime – remain as unsolved as ever. Who on earth was Eustache Dauger?

To find the answer, we must go looking for Eustache in the outside world. But first, there are the clues he left behind him in prison – a relationship with Nicolas Fouquet, the disgraced finance minister, who knew Dauger's secret already from the days before 1661, and quite possibly knew Dauger as well; and an unexplained link between the crime that led to Dauger's arrest in 1669, and the Count of Lauzun, who was not allowed to know that Dauger was even at Pignerol. It is these two men whose prison lives must now be examined, to see what we can turn up that will lead us closer to the secret of the man in the mask.

Notes on Chapter 14

1 Like Dauger, Mattioli was to be put in one of the two new vaulted cells.

15

Prisoners of d'Artagnan

Nicolas Fouquet, finance minister, and Antoine Nompar de Caumont, the Marquis de Puyguilhem and Count of Lauzun, were both important prisoners of state. Prisoners so important that they were taken to the most far-flung prison in the land by the famous d'Artagnan himself. Fouquet's crime was well known: he had embezzled millions from the public finances and built himself great palaces on the proceeds. He had invited the king to banquets more lavish than anything the king could afford himself. It had taken d'Artagnan to arrest him and a three-year trial to bring him down. But Lauzun, on the other hand, had done nothing. Indeed, he had only recently been mysteriously promoted. The riddle of Lauzun's arrest was the talk of the royal court. Lauzun himself, locked in Pignerol, threw himself around his cell, raged in disbelief at his punishment and begged to be told what he had done. St Mars, of course, did not know the answer either. But he could probably have hazarded a guess that it was not unconnected with the fate of the iron mask. One wonders why d'Artagnan was not also given the task of arresting Dauger: perhaps the great man would have had nothing to do with so apparently cruel a punishment as Louvois and the king had dreamed up for the hapless prisoner from Dunkirk.

Of the two prisoners he did conduct to Pignerol, Fouquet was the first, arrested in 1661. The word 'Fouquet' comes

from a local French dialect and means 'squirrel'. Nicolas
Fouquet displayed an autobiographical climbing squirrel
on his coat of arms, with the Latin motto 'Quo non
ascendam?' meaning 'To what heights may I not climb?'
As a statement of intent it was obvious. For many years in
France, it had become the custom for the country to be
ruled in reality by a powerful chief minister, while the king
did little or nothing. The more famous was Cardinal
Richelieu, who controlled the feeble Louis XIII; after him
came his protégé, Cardinal Mazarin. After Mazarin's death
in March 1661, Fouquet was expected to take over the
helm, as the protégé of both the cardinals. But the young
Louis XIV was an utterly different proposition from his
father. He wanted to break the chain and rule himself, and
there were plenty of rival ministers willing to help him
bring Fouquet down. As Fouquet struggled to consolidate
his new position as the foremost minister in the land, the
king struck, abetted by Michel le Tellier, the father of
Louvois, and by Colbert, another familiar face.

The trap was simple – so simple that it is surprising how
easily Fouquet fell for it. Everybody knew that Fouquet
had been embezzling state finances for years – he was the
richest man in the country. But he had protected himself
by securing the office of procureur-général, who could only
be tried by Parliament, and then by stuffing Parliament
with his own men. He also owned a ring of fortresses
around the country for good measure. Unfortunately he
wanted the elusive prime minister's job too much and too
soon for his own good. On the grounds that one man would
be too busy to do both jobs, Louis offered him the prime
ministership on condition that he resign as procureur-
général, and Fouquet accepted. On 17 August 1661 Fouquet held a magnificent ball at his new Château of Vaux to
celebrate. It was a sumptuous occasion, costing over
£20,000. Diamonds were handed out free to all the guests.
But it also proved to be Nicolas Fouquet's farewell party.
Before he could leave Vaux, he was arrested by d'Artagnan
and charged with corruption. Simultaneously, his castles

were stormed by battalions of royal troops. His replacement at the finance ministry, who had already begun preparing the evidence against him for his trial, was Colbert.

For three years Fouquet was guarded by d'Artagnan and his number two, a dependable musketeer captain named St Mars, while eminent judges debated the case. Gaoling Fouquet was not going to be easy. He was an influential man. In spite of all his misdeeds, he was a lovable rogue and the powerful Parisian crowd was right behind him. Furthermore, he had 'proofs' of his innocence prepared for just such an eventuality. But Louis was determined to remove any threat to his own power: all Fouquet's papers, anything that could be used in his defence, were seized and destroyed. In their place appeared forged documents, detailing his supposed affairs with the current royal mistress, Louise de la Vallière. Louis was determined on a death sentence.

Louis XIV has sometimes been painted as a noble man, even kindly; but he had a vicious, vindictive, murderous streak. The only thing that frightened him was the crowd, and it was this that saved Fouquet. The judges voted only to banish Fouquet to another country; Louis was furious, but he dared not overturn the decision because of Fouquet's popularity. Instead he consoled himself with 'commuting' Fouquet's sentence to life imprisonment, and revenging himself upon the judges and Fouquet's family. Fouquet knew too much to be allowed to leave France at liberty; he must go to Pignerol. The king said: 'It would not be safe to let Fouquet go out of the kingdom, seeing the great knowledge he possesses of the most important state affairs.' Cheering, waving crowds lined the route to Pignerol, to wish Fouquet well on his way.

For many years, Nicolas Fouquet was thought to have been the masked man; indeed, he still is supposed to be, in some quarters. There are reference books that identify him as the masked prisoner. Exactly why anyone should have wanted to mask Fouquet and prevent him from being recognised as a prisoner, when the whole of Paris had

applauded him on his way to gaol, is a mystery. But the
theory arose from various contemporary suggestions that
his sentence was really a punishment for having dallied
with one or more royal mistresses. In fact a card, found in
the Bastille in 1789, referred to Fouquet's arrival from
Sainte-Marguerite in an iron mask. This was later shown
to be a poor forgery. Interestingly, soon after the masked
man's death, the diarist St Simon wrote that Fouquet had
been gaoled at Pignerol for a total of thirty-four years – the
exact figure that Dauger, the real masked man, spent in
prison. This cannot be a coincidence: it must have slipped
through the security net somehow, or be part of the royal
disinformation campaign. But it certainly was not Fouquet,
who spent only nineteen years in custody, that died in the
Bastille in 1703.

We should at least establish Fouquet's alibi. To start
with, November 1703 would have been the forty-third year
of Fouquet's imprisonment; and not only that, he would
have been 88, rather older than the descriptions of the
masked man that we possess would indicate. His imprisonment, as we have seen, was no secret. There was of course
the occasion in 1665 when he had briefly been billeted in
the town, at the house of a Monsieur Damorezan, after a
thunderbolt had blown up the gunpowder magazine.[1] His
security precautions were nothing like those of the masked
man. And perhaps most convincingly, his death was well
attested in 1680. A letter written by Louvois on 8 April
1680 refers to 'the death of Monsieur Fouquet'. Another,
written in April 1684, refers to 'the late Monsieur Fouquet'
and St Mars uses the same phrase in January 1696. In fact,
Fouquet died in the presence not only of St Mars but of his
entire family, who by 1680 were allowed to visit him. They
even took his body away a few weeks later.

Fouquet was not the masked man. But what is important
is the fact that he was allowed to meet Eustache Dauger
and talk to him freely, as no-one else was, suggesting that
Dauger's secret must have been known to Fouquet before
his arrest in 1661. Fouquet had been the most important

minister in the country; before that, as Richelieu's and
Mazarin's right-hand man, he had known every state secret
there was to know. What is intriguing is not that he knew
the secret, but that it was obviously an old one. It has been
established how Fouquet was trusted with the secret in
Pignerol because his only way out of prison and back to
favour was to co-operate with the king, keep himself to
himself and offer information to the authorities: how Fouquet was expected, in 1678, to know all about Eustache's
'past life', whereas St Mars was not, and to report whether
La Rivière had learnt anything about it; and how he was
rewarded for his co-operation, with visits from his family
and from local prostitutes. Fouquet himself had offered his
services to the king as early as 1673 in order to reveal or
discuss 'a secret': perhaps they were discussing Dauger
even then? At any rate, it is clear that Fouquet was trusted
to hold his tongue.

Furthermore, he was generally a well-behaved prisoner.
At first, he had been mischievous, making ink from soot
and wine, and pens from chicken bones, and hiding them
in the back of his chair. St Mars said he made 'excellent
paper, on which I used to let him write, and then later I
used to take it at night from the little pocket he had made
at the bottom of his breeches.' But Fouquet was something
of a poet, and these writings were hardly scurrilous; after
1673 he was officially given pen and paper to save him the
bother, and was allowed to write to his wife. By 1672, St
Mars was reporting that Fouquet was 'as patient and well-
behaved as Lauzun is furious'.

As the king's man, then, and with no real option to
choose otherwise, Fouquet would not have left us any clues
deliberately. But in death Fouquet could not be so careful,
and has left us an important clue. Fouquet died on 23
March 1680. The official reason, according to the *Gazette de
France*, was 'a sudden attack of apoplexy'. Fouquet had a
history of high blood pressure into the bargain. But the
matter was discussed in letters between Pignerol and Paris

throughout the Spring, and on 10 July 1680 comes perhaps the most mysterious letter of all. Louvois ordered St Mars:

> Report to me how it is possible that the man named Eustache has done that which you told me about, and where he got the drugs necessary to do it, as I cannot believe that you would have furnished them to him.

Paris obviously felt this to be a staggeringly important episode. So important, in fact, that Louvois wrote out the letter himself, in his own hand. Even his trusted personal secretary, who wrote all his correspondence, had not to see it.

The second of the two questions asked – 'where Eustache got the drugs necessary to do it' – can be answered, for Fouquet had always distrusted the surgeon of the citadel, and was allowed to compound his own remedies. He was obviously fond of home medicine, for he had taught himself the art of dispensing. But what had Eustache actually done with these drugs? Had he poisoned Fouquet? It sounds extremely far-fetched, but there are possible pointers to it. First, the symptoms of Fouquet's death, as witnessed by his family and subsequently recorded by Madame de Sévigné, exactly corresponded to those of a poisoned man – 'convulsions and heart pains without being able to vomit'. Secondly, Fouquet's body was not handed over to his family immediately, as would have been the normal procedure, but on the 9 April, seventeen days after his death: just the right amount of time for traces of poison to disappear from the body. Add to this the secrecy attached to the episode by Louvois, and you have an extraordinary possibility. What it does prove either way is that in Dauger we are looking for a man who had some affinity with drugs and chemicals. What it might prove, also, although we cannot know for sure, is that he was a man who could make or use poisons.

The affair of the drugs was not the only stir caused by Fouquet's death. St Mars, already in trouble for allowing Fouquet's son to remove his poems and other papers, evidently found some other papers of a more serious nature; but he waited two months – until 8 June – before sending them. Louvois replied on the 22nd:

> With regard to the loose sheet which accompanied your letter of the 8th, you were wrong not to report what it contained to me on the very first day that you knew of it. In addition, I bid you to send me, in a parcel, what you found in the pockets of Monsieur Fouquet, so that I can present it to his Majesty.

What these objects and papers were, is not known. They were not the only discovery made by the embarrassed St Mars. For, upon clearing out Fouquet's cell, he discovered that the apparently solid bars in the chimney had been cut through. Lauzun had made a tunnel into Fouquet's cell, in order to visit him at night. Louvois wrote:

> His Majesty has commanded me to let you know, that after you have had the hole through which Messieurs Fouquet and Lauzun communicated with each other without your knowledge blocked up, and this remade so solidly that it will not be possible to work at this spot . . . you should persuade Monsieur de Lauzun that the man named Eustache d'Augers, and the said La Rivière, have been set at liberty . . .

Again, it is not known what passed on these nocturnal visits. Lauzun was allowed to see Fouquet anyway during the day. Dauger was always withdrawn from Fouquet's cell on these occasions, but he was also returned to his own cell every night, so we can be sure that Lauzun was not meeting Dauger on these visits. Presumably he discussed Dauger with Fouquet, but it is doubtful whether Fouquet told him anything of importance. The two men cordially disliked each other. At any rate, the king and Louvois were taking no chances. It was after these episodes that Eustache and his companion lost their identity and became simply 'the gentlemen of the lower tower', forbidden ever to see or speak to anybody again. Security was intensified, and soon afterwards they were transferred to Exiles.

The Count of Lauzun and Fouquet had got on very badly during their visiting periods. Typically, Lauzun had tried to seduce Fouquet's daughter when her father was ill. But more importantly, the ex-finance minister just couldn't believe or understand how the poor Gascon cadet who had come to cadge money from him as a young man could possibly have risen to become Captain of the King's Bodyguard. It was an extraordinary promotion for a man who was socially destined for lower things; and it was made doubly intriguing by the fact that Lauzun had been promoted on 28 July 1669, *the exact day when the King sent Captain Vauroy at Dunkirk the orders to arrest Dauger*.

Antoine de Caumont, Count of Lauzun, was an outrageous, rude and exhibitionistic provincial parvenu. He was cool and courageous too, but he took too many risks and alienated a great many people. He could be mean, malicious, reckless, disrespectful and difficult. Generally, he was dismissed as a mere upstart. 'It is not lawful even to dream as this man lived,' wrote La Bruyère, and La Fare called him 'the most insolent little man who had been seen for a century'. But Lauzun often found his way into favour, only to lose it again due to some reckless act. His first real brush with authority came in 1665 when he fell for the same young lady as the king – the Princess of Monaco. He hid in a closet to overhear their conversation and was given a spell in the Bastille for his pains. Then, early in 1669, he persuaded the king to give him the job of Master of the Artillery. Hardly had he begun to celebrate his impending appointment, when the enemies of the upstart Gascon moved to unseat him. Persuaded by Louvois and the new royal mistress, Madame de Montespan, the king reversed his decision. Lauzun was outraged. He called Montespan 'a liar and a bitch', and threatened to tear out her eyes, when she claimed to have supported him. Montespan became convinced that he was the devil, because he was able to repeat to her every detail of her conversation with the king. Louis knew better: Lauzun had been hiding under their bed.[2] In the furious interview that followed, Lauzun broke his sword over his knee and said that he 'would never serve a King who broke his word on the advice of a whore'. Louis sent him back to the Bastille, for another spell behind bars.

It was from these depths that Lauzun suddenly, inexplicably, bounced back to the premier position of Captain of the King's Bodyguard. The diarist St Simon described Lauzun's unexpected advancement:

> Here was an absolute miracle . . . the King released Lauzun from the Bastille, then communicated with him through intermediaries, and eventually received him, and at once made him Captain of the Royal Bodyguard! . . . The Artillery was given to the Count of Lude, who was the existing Captain of the Bodyguard, who was seriously inconvenienced by his demotion . . . all this took place inside six weeks. What a turnaround for an ambitious man, and what a sensation in the court!

The courtiers were as amazed as they were envious. What could Lauzun have done to change the position so? Nobody could account for it. Other rewards followed thick and fast: the 'Grandes Entrées de la Cour', an extraordinary favour which gave free access throughout the royal quarters, and the governorship of Berry. Then – just as suddenly – came an even more astonishing body blow.

> King Louis xiv to St Mars, 20.10.71. Monsieur de St Mars, I am writing this letter to tell you that my intention is to send to my citadel of Pignerol the Count of Lauzun, Captain of my Bodyguard, to be carefully guarded there, and that as soon as the Sieur d'Artagnan, Captain-Lieutenant of the first company of Musketeers of my guard, whom I have charged with the conduct of the said Count of Lauzun, has arrived at my said citadel, you will receive the said Count of Lauzun yourself, and keep him under good and secure guard until any new

order of mine, without permitting him to communicate
with anyone, neither by word or by letter.

Nobody was allowed to speak to him or to see him, none of
his friends were to be allowed to visit him. He was forced
to resign his position. From being one of the most influential
men in the land, Lauzun had become just another prisoner
at Pignerol. The papal ambassador in Paris reported the
controversy to Rome: 'The motive for imprisonment has
not been published . . . one waits for the news that His
Majesty has found in Lauzun's papers letters that will
convict him of high treason.' A later Count of Lauzun
wrote: 'The Gazette d'Amsterdam pondered the reasons for
the catastrophe, as did all Europe, without being able to
shed any light on the mystery.' St Simon added: 'This
mystery has never been cleared up.'

Some historians have hopefully attributed Lauzun's
arrest to the fact that he had become engaged to the King's
cousin[3], supposedly enraging Louis XIV. As this had happened a whole year previously, the King's rage was
obviously a slow burning emotion.

The only inference it is possible to make is that Lauzun's
sudden promotion had been linked to the simultaneous
arrest of Eustache Dauger on 28 July 1669, and that his
equally sudden fall came when he gave the King some
reason to trust him no longer. Dauger, remember, seems to
have been trying to flee the country in 1669 and had almost
certainly been betrayed to the authorities. Lauzun was just
the kind of man to betray a friend to the king in return for
advancement. St Simon wrote:

> He had a fine valour, but unbounded ambition, and a
> malicious streak which could refuse no incentive . . . his
> magnificent exterior could not hide feelings of greed. He
> was always occupied by schemes, and more often by wild
> dreams . . . he had a fine physionomy, with a smile which
> demonstrated both depth and treachery.

La Bruyère added: 'He was unburdened with money or
scruples, and determined to push his way to the front.'

Perhaps the king was now merely leaving a discreet interval before arresting Lauzun too, or perhaps Lauzun had pushed the royal goodwill too far, in the hope of further advancement. Whichever it was, the king – so terrified of Dauger's secret – was also just the kind of man to go in for doublecross, and lock Lauzun up to be on the safe side, just in case he had learnt anything from his wheeling and dealing. That he had not was obvious from his rage and astonishment at being imprisoned. But whatever he did know, we must now suspect that the masked man was a friend or colleague of his. This would surely explain why Lauzun and Dauger were forbidden to discover that the other was imprisoned in Pignerol: Louis would want to confine the three men who might know something (Fouquet being the other) under one roof and to one gaoler, but within their prison Dauger and Lauzun must obviously be kept apart.

Lauzun was just the man to test St Mars to the full. Louvois warned the gaoler:

Be much more on the alert guarding this prisoner than has been necessary for [Fouquet], because he is capable of doing very much more to escape by strength, or cleverness, or by corrupting someone, than is Monsieur Fouquet.

St Mars replied, overconfidently:

I will lodge him in the two lower cells which are underneath those of Monsieur Fouquet: these are the ones with the window grills and heavy iron bars that you yourself saw. From what I am having done in this place, I can answer to you with my life for the security of Monsieur de Lauzun, and also for the fact that he can neither receive nor send any news to the outside. I stake my honour, Sir, that while this gentleman is under my guard, you will never again hear any news about him. I will take all my precautions so well and be so alert that I will fail in none of my promises. You have made His

Majesty's will so clear as regards the security of this new prisoner, that it will be as if he already rested in peace. I will treat him honestly without, however, having any communication with him, unless you expressly command it. The place that I am preparing is so constructed that I can have holes made, to spy into his apartments. I intend to know all that he does and says in every detail, through the reports of the valet whom I will give him as you ordered . . . Never will Monsieur Fouquet know that he has a companion.

Inside his barred, screened cell, Lauzun could not believe what had happened. St Mars wrote:

I do not believe, Sir, that I can report any news of my prisoner's being quieter: he is in so profound a grief that he does nothing other than sigh and beat his feet [against the ground]; he eats very little . . . He asked me once if I knew the cause of his detention; I said to him that I never learnt news of this kind.

Lauzun threatened to kill himself. St Mars reported again:

As I do not stop to listen to his rantings, he reproached me that I had become hard and pitiless due to the length of my service as a gaoler, and said that he had never been officially sentenced and that his worst punishment was that he is ignorant of his crime . . . I cannot tell you how great his displeasure and sorrow are; he is in despair at being at Pignerol under my guard.

The precautions taken to secure Lauzun began to rival those made on Dauger's behalf. St Mars wrote:

I shall not fail to have the linen you are sending me for Lauzun thoroughly wet, after having every seam examined; anything written upon the linen will vanish, when it is wet. Everything which is brought out of his room is put in a tub full of water after being examined, and the laundress bringing it from the river dries it before the fire in front of my officers, who take this duty in turns, week by week. I also take this precaution with the napkins.

Lauzun retaliated by burning a hole in the floorboards of his cell. Louvois was not satisfied.

> When Monsieur de Lauzun burnt a plank in the floor of his room, it was certainly to see what was underneath; and if such a thing happens again, you must speak severely to him, and declare that you will have him guarded continually. Moreover, you should pay him frequent visits; you should often look under the bed to see he has not lifted boards to try to escape that way, and should, moreover, take all the other precautions that you can.

Lauzun went through bouts of fury and periods of mysticism. He went on hunger strikes and refused to wash. He became a religious maniac and refused to shave, until his beard reached epic proportions. He smashed his furniture, set fire to his room and physically attacked St Mars. Sent a Capucin monk as a confessor, he tried to yank the man's beard off in the conviction that he was a spy. When he went out for his daily exercise, three gaolers and six armed guards went with him in case he needed to be restrained.

Then, to add to the mystery, one of Lauzun's servants – named Heurtault – was arrested near Pignerol. He killed himself before he could be made to talk, but papers found upon him revealed that Mathonnet, one of the guards, had been bribed to help Lauzun escape. Mathonnet was arrested. Paris went into a flurry of panic, and although in the middle of a war with Holland, Louvois turned his complete attention to the case. St Mars was ordered to round up each one of the plotters and to make them talk 'through any means, no matter what'. In the 1670s this meant being torn in half on the rack or filled with water literally to bursting point. St Mars carried out the orders. 'I have only to find the smallest charge against a soldier or domestic,' he said, 'and I shall hang him at once.' And that, he confirmed, included any of his relatives on the staff. Paris had to know whether anyone had spoken to Lauzun. 'I cannot swear that an attempt has not been made', wrote St Mars, 'but I can pledge my life in the assurance that the effort has not been successful.'

In 1676 Lauzun almost succeeded in escaping. After three years of scraping and scratching, he finally made a hole in the stone underfloor of his room with a bent nail; he dropped into the vault below, removed the bars on the window and climbed down into the moat on a rope ladder made of table napkins. From there he burrowed into the courtyard of the citadel as dawn broke, and walked slap bang into a servant. Louvois was furious. He wanted to know how Lauzun could apparently tear Pignerol down brick by brick without anyone noticing. For the embarrassed St Mars, the episode was the start of many a lonely and uncomfortable afternoon spent hidden in the branches of a pear tree opposite Lauzun's cell, attempting to spy on him.

Just like Dauger, just like Fouquet, Lauzun was kept securely in Pignerol and given everything he wanted. Louvois wrote to him personally to say that St Mars had 'orders to give you all things necessary in life that you desire, and never to fail in according the respect which is due to your birth and to the rank which you have held at court.'

But there was one very surprising difference in the treatment of Lauzun. For, unlike Fouquet and unlike the masked man, Lauzun was eventually released. At first sight this appears incomprehensible, in view of the security precautions taken to prevent him seeing or speaking to anyone. But there are a number of possible explanations.

First, the continuing imprisonment of Lauzun was an enormous public embarrassment. It was still the topic of conversation at court. Voltaire wrote that 'during the whole of his reign, [Louis XIV] committed no act of such a nature . . . of such severity [as this]'. This is an exaggeration, but it demonstrates the depth of feeling about the affair.

Dauger's arrest had been a secret. Fouquet's incarceration was for a good reason, but Lauzun had manifestly committed no crime. What is more, the Princess Mademoiselle de Montpensier, the royal cousin who had become engaged to Lauzun a year before his arrest, had some influence with the King. Although she was immensely rich and several years Lauzun's senior, a suspicious betrothal entirely in keeping with what we know of his character, she obviously held a great deal of affection for him. For a decade she had been begging, badgering and beseeching Louis to release her fiancé, or at least explain what he was doing in prison. By 1681, this was even more of a public embarrassment than it had been in 1671. She had even handed over much of her wealth to the king in the hope of engineering his release.

Then, more importantly, there is the fact that Louis and Louvois obviously became convinced that Lauzun did not share the masked man's secret. In fact, a distinct change came about in their attitude when Fouquet started to pass information to them. Fouquet and Lauzun were allowed to meet, and Fouquet obviously made it clear to the king that Lauzun was as innocent as he had protested so loudly for so long. The episode of Fouquet's death demonstrates clearly that Paris was fully aware of the extent of Lauzun's knowledge. For when Fouquet died, it was decided to transfer the gentlemen of the tower to Exiles. Lauzun did not go with them. Instead St Mars was ordered, as we have seen, 'to persuade Monsieur de Lauzun that the man named Eustache d'Augers, and the said La Rivière, have been set at liberty'. Now Lauzun was not supposed to know that Dauger was at Pignerol – but he obviously did, and Paris was obviously aware of this. But if Lauzun really had known Dauger's secret, then there would be no point in trying to persuade him that Dauger had been freed – for he would know that the secret was so important that Dauger could never be freed. So the implication is that although he knew of Dauger's presence, and that Dauger had committed some crime conceivably worthy of a twelve-year sentence, Lauzun was as ignorant of the real importance of the

whole matter as he made out. As a further illustration of
his innocence, Lauzun's valet was released with him – in
stark contrast to Fouquet's valet, the unhappy La Rivière,
who was known to have learnt the secret and so shared
Dauger's fate.

Once Dauger and La Rivière had been transferred after
Fouquet's death, Lauzun was called to Paris for a lengthy
interview with Louvois. The intention, presumably, was to
remove any doubts about his innocence and to make it
quite clear what would happen if he was indiscreet. He was
'compensated' for his stay in prison, to the tune of £1000,
and freed on certain conditions. These conditions included
living in a room with barred windows under house arrest
in Amboise, being banned from coming within several miles
of Paris, and being attended everywhere by his own personal guard – Captain de Maupertuis of the musketeers, a
friend and confidant of St Mars – who was to make sure
that Lauzun behaved himself. But Lauzun was not too
unhappy. He inherited all the old lady's money when she
died, and married St Simon's fifteen-year-old sister-in-law
when he was sixty-three. Eventually he was allowed to join
the army, where he helped to stage-manage the flight of the
deposed James ii's family from England, and led the
defeated French forces at the Battle of the Boyne in Ireland.
He was captured by the British, and among his papers they
found nine letters addressed to him and signed by Louvois,
written in code. Whether they have any bearing on the
mystery of the man in the iron mask is not known. To this
day they have never been deciphered, but they still repose
in the British Museum. If you would like to have a try, an
extract is reprinted in the Appendix.

The story of the masked prisoner has weaved uncertainly
in and out of the chequered careers of Antoine, Count of
Lauzun and Nicolas Fouquet. But we have been left with a
reasonable probability that Lauzun betrayed our man in
some way, presumably by alerting the authorities to his
whereabouts in return for promotion, and that he was
imprisoned in Pignerol in the mistaken fear that he might

know the masked man's secret. The authorities may have learnt of their error from Fouquet, who had himself known the secret before 1661. As it has been established, the fact that the secret was an old one suggests that either Dauger had just learnt it and could not be trusted with it, or that he had always known it and was now trying to misuse it.

Perhaps Dauger had tried to enlist Lauzun as an accomplice in such a crime? Whether or not this was the case, Eustache Dauger was probably a friend or acquaintance of Lauzun, possibly also of Fouquet. So we must hunt among the friends of Lauzun. We are looking for a man handy with drugs and chemicals: a Frenchman, Catholic, well-built, well-travelled and well-bred, although perhaps someone fallen on hard times. We know that he was born around the late 1630s, disappeared without trace in 1669, and that he bore a strong resemblance to somebody – probably the king. We know that his name really was Eustache Dauger. It is not a description that could apply to many people.

Notes on Chapter 15

1 Fouquet obviously led a charmed life: his entire cell was blown to smithereens except for the window alcove where he was standing, watching the storm.
2 One hopes that it was a strong bed, for Lauzun's sake. As he had got older, the King had become grossly fat.
3 The Princess Mademoiselle de Montpensier, daughter of Gaston of Orléans, brother of the king's father, Louis XIII.

16

The black sheep of the family

Where does one start looking for a Dauger? Obviously the
first place to look is under the letter 'D' in any alphabetical
records. There are a few. There was a gentleman by the
name of Gilbert Daugers who was Louis XIV's steward in
1652 – a gentleman valet – but he is rather too old for us.
And, to cheer those who would have us believe that the
masked man was a priest, the Archbishop of Sens, the uncle
of the royal mistress Madame de Montespan, had a chaplain called Daugé in 1670. But he could hardly have been
arrested in 1669. In fact, neither man disappeared without
trace – somebody would certainly have noticed if they had
– and neither man bore the name 'Eustache'.

This name 'Eustache Dauger' presents a problem. It is
undoubtedly a real name, otherwise it would not have been
necessary to scratch it off royal documents, leave it out of
records altogether, or replace it with a false name such as
Marchioly. Yet there do not seem to have been any
Eustache Daugers alive in France at the time, so there must
be a catch somewhere. We do have two clues to go on. The
first is that Dauger could have been a friend of Lauzun.
The second is provided for us by Louvois himself. For in
that illuminating letter of 8 April 1680, Louvois told St
Mars 'to persuade Monsieur de Lauzun that the man
named Eustache d'Augers, and the said La Rivière, have
been set at liberty'. Now for eleven years, Louvois had
referred to Eustache as 'Dauger': he never varied. Of course

it was an age of vague and imprecise spelling, but this was
the only time that Louvois ever referred to the prisoner as
'd'Augers'. St Mars had used the name 'd'Auger' once,
when his prisoner had first arrived, but thereafter he had
taken his cue from Paris and used the word 'Dauger' as
well. The implication of this is that Lauzun would know
the prisoner as Eustache d'Augers, Eustache *of* Augers, and
not as Dauger. Suddenly we find ourselves looking under
the letter 'A', and asking whether Lauzun had a friend
called Augers in the years leading up to 1669.

Lauzun does seem to have had one particular friend, one
kindred spirit, the kind of irresponsible soul ready to dive
heartily into brawls and other youthful escapades with him.
According to the Count of Brienne, Lauzun and this friend
were always squabbling with each other, but at heart they
were inseparable, 'each one as mad as the other'. The name
of the friend was Cavoye. The Cavoyes were an aristocratic
family from Picardy who had made a mark for themselves
at court; in later years, Louis de Cavoye rose to become the
King's closest companion. But the name 'Cavoye' here did
not refer to Louis de Cavoye. Louis was the fifth of six
brothers, and the simple term 'Cavoye' was customarily
reserved for the eldest brother. The eldest Cavoye brother
was Pierre, born in 1627. But Pierre was not Lauzun's
special friend either. For the Count of Brienne was describing what Lauzun was like in 1655, and Pierre de Cavoye
had been killed in action at Lens in 1648. The second
brother, Charles, had also been killed in action, in 1654. So
by 1655, the eldest of the Cavoyes and Lauzun's inseparable friend was the third brother, born in 1637 – Eustache
de Cavoye. The little used family name of the Cavoye
family was Auger. So Eustache's full name was Eustache
d'Auger de Cavoye. And he was last heard of in 1668, at
the age of 30. We have found our man.

It was a brilliantly simple trick. Louvois and the King
had incarcerated the hapless Eustache under his family
name, rather as if somebody now were to hide the Duke of
Westminster under the name 'Gerald Grosvenor'. There is

even one copy of Eustache's signature surviving, where he has actually signed himself 'dauger de Cavoy'. But what had Eustache done? And how could such a potentially important nobleman disappear without trace, without anybody noticing or complaining? To understand, we must look into the story of Eustache and the Cavoye family. And as the story unfolds, each successive detail confirms that Eustache d'Auger de Cavoye must indeed have been the man in the iron mask.

The house of Auger was one of the oldest in France – descended from Ogier the Dane, one of the twelve Lords of Charlemagne in the eighth century. In the fourteenth century they were granted the lands of Cavoye, which lay around the village of Epagny and the castle of Beaufort-en-Santerre, and they settled down to become rural lords of the manor. Ironically, Eustache's grandfather, Adrien de Cavoye, was known as 'the man with the iron arm'. But it was not until the birth of Adrien's son François around 1600 that the Cavoye family came back into its former glory. François was a great French hero, the d'Artagnan of his day; a fine swordsman and duellist, who came to court to make his fortune with his blade and rose to become the first ever captain of Cardinal Richelieu's musketeers in 1634.[1] The dashing captain had taken as his wife Marie de Serignan, a noted 21-year-old beauty from the Languedoc. In an age of adultery and scandal it was considered to be the perfect marriage. He was courageous and noble, she was attractive, clever and witty; both were popular, both were influential, both were utterly faithful to Richelieu and the crown. The French historian Adrien Huguet described them as a model couple:

> At the time when the laws of marriage were suffering, and when so many illegitimate unions overtly manifested themselves . . . at the same period when, to follow a ridiculous perversion of fashion, so many honest women feigned the existence of a lover so as not to appear to be left out, Monsieur and Madame de Cavoye displayed an almost impertinent degree of conjugal bliss.

When he was away, she wrote to him up to three times a day. According to a friend, she still wept for him twenty years after his death.

François remained at the top of his profession and remained Richelieu's favourite until his career was slightly dented in 1640. As head of the cardinal's musketeers he was held responsible for the royal rancour that had resulted from an unseemly brawl in the town centre of Treville. In fact, the fight had started when a group of the cardinal's musketeers had been provoked by a slightly tipsy young royal musketeer on his first day of service, named d'Artagnan. Three others had rushed to his defence, named Athos, Porthos and Aramis, which was to become the beginning of a famous friendship.[2]

But for six years before 1640, François de Cavoye held undisputed sway. And just as he was Richelieu's right-hand man, so Marie became the Queen's friend and lady-in-waiting. The marriage was extremely fertile: eleven children were born to the couple, and all the boys followed their father into military service. François de Cavoye was killed in action, serving his King and his Cardinal at the Siege of Bapaume in September 1641. The notification reached Marie thus:

19th September

The Sieur de Cavoye, Captain of the Company of Musketeers belonging to His Eminence, died the day before yesterday of wounds that he had received while leading the assault on the trenches at Bapaume.

She broke down and wept.

All François' sons – except two – followed their father to a soldier's grave, although he never lived to see them grow to manhood. In some respects he was fortunate: for he never lived to see the unpleasant creature he had created in Eustache. Eustache was born in the inappropriately named Rue des Bons Enfants in Paris, a stone's throw from the royal palace, on 30 August 1637. He was baptised eighteen months later in the parish of St Eustache, from which he

Signatures of the Cavoye brothers, using the form 'Dauger de Cavoy'.

took his name. As a young man, he was part of a tightly-knit circle of friends, some of whose identities will come as no surprise. There were the Cavoye boys; there was the young King Louis XIV, now risen to the throne but as yet very much under the control of Cardinal Mazarin; there was Philip Mancini, Mazarin's nephew; there was the Count of Lauzun; there was Madame de Montespan's brother, the Count of Vivonne; and there was Cyrano de Bergerac. A golden future lay ahead of them, for their adult protectors were influential, and included Queen Anne, Louis XIV's mother; Cardinal Mazarin, who like Richelieu was very close to the Cavoyes; a neighbour of the Cavoyes, Jean-Baptiste Colbert, later to be minister of finances; and another rising star of politics, who was in fact a relative of the Cavoye family – a young man named Nicolas Fouquet. But the Cavoye family had some dedicated enemies as well. As she grew older and became the royal mistress, there was Montespan. And in particular, there was another rising star and friend of the king: his name was the Marquis de Louvois.

All the chief protagonists in the mystery are coming together and revealing the links that connect them at last. Louvois, Eustache's enemy, who was so determined to make life worse for the masked man. Colbert, Eustache's family friend, who never discovered the masked man's name or existence because all mention of him was torn out of the register which required Colbert's signature. Fouquet, Eustache's relative, who was allowed to see this 'valet' in prison. The ambitious Lauzun, Eustache's boyhood friend, who betrayed him to the authorities. And King Louis xiv, who despite the obvious enormity of whatever crime Eustache had committed, insisted on keeping him alive and in decent conditions: for Louis, too, was Eustache's friend. The Count of Brienne tells us of an occasion when Eustache and Lauzun started fighting right behind the King's back in the middle of a procession down the staircase of the Louvre, and Eustache's wig fell to the ground in the struggle. Furious, the King turned round, but Brienne stepped between them with his cloak. 'I thank you', said the King to Brienne, 'for having spared me the trouble of being angered against and punishing a person I love.'

As Eustache grew up, he must have become more and more difficult to love. Despite the fact that the path to success was ready made for him to follow, he became the black sheep of the family with a vengeance. All the Cavoye boys joined the crack Guards regiment – Eustache in 1652. His eldest brother Pierre had been killed in 1648, and the second brother Charles had died at Arras in 1654, fighting alongside Cyrano de Bergerac, so by the age of 27 Eustache was due to inherit the Lordship of Cavoye. He never did. On Good Friday of 1659 a group of devil-worshippers were caught celebrating a black mass in the chapel of the Château of Roissy. Robed in black, they had christened a pig in the place of Jesus Christ and roasted it. There was also a homosexual element in the 'service'. The scandal was terrible, for among their number were Eustache de Cavoye,[3] his friends Vivonne and Mancini, and the King's chaplain, the Abbot Camus. A horrified d'Artagnan was reported to have said about the episode:

They mocked the two most august sacraments that we possess in our religion: the baptism and the eucharist;

terrible things have emerged from that episode which are best left unspoken, even forgotten entirely. In fact one can neither talk about it nor remember it without a feeling of horror, so the best thing is never to talk about it . . .

Another contemporary account stated: 'They did things that are repugnant not only to Christians but to any persons of sensitivity.'

The careers of everyone present were broken – except Eustache. Only the Cavoye family had the clout for Eustache to survive. On the very same day that Bussy-Rabutin, the eldest reveller present, was sent into permanent exile, the prime minister himself, Cardinal Mazarin, wrote personally to Eustache's mother to tell her that the king had decided to take no action against her son: 'I beg you to believe that you have no servant more devoted than myself, as you and all your family will always see.'

Eustache went on to be promoted in 1662. By 1661 he had the two fiefs of Calvant and Montvilliers to himself and a healthy income of £600 a year, and was already being referred to as 'The Lord of Cavoye' (behind his back, however, he was nicknamed 'Roissy', after the site of his exploits).

But Eustache had obviously not learnt his lesson. Sometime in early 1664, he did something else so terrible that his mother disinherited him, 'for good causes and considerations known to her'. She cut herself off from him completely. According to the custom of Picardy, it was written into Marie's marriage contract that she had the right to decide which of her sons would become Lord of Cavoye. Now she decided to exercise this right and override Eustache's natural claims. Instead she chose Louis, her third surviving son, to succeed to the title. Louis de Cavoye soon became King Louis xiv's best friend and Grand Master of the Royal Household; Eustache moved out of the family home in the Rue Vivienne.

The great d'Artagnan was said to have spoken in

scathing terms about Eustache's character: he was, we are told, 'one who brought shame to his brother, one who enjoyed playing the swashbuckler a little too much'. When Eustache was around, 'one could see clashing swords in the worst places, on the flimsiest of excuses'. Further clues to Eustache's character may be gleaned from a packet found in poor Marie's effects after her death, in July 1665: it contained 'seventy-five documents, receipts for payments made to various people by the deceased lady, for Monsieur Eustache d'Auger de Cavoye, her son'. Marie was paying off his debts. Eustache was squandering the family fortune.

Soon he became more and more desperate for money. His mother had provided him with £1000 a year on top of his existing £600, but it was not enough. He sold his two fiefs to his brother Louis and formally abandoned all hereditary rights to the Cavoye wealth, for £400 a year. He still had his officer's commission in the army: but that was not to last for long. In June 1665 Eustache became involved in a drunken argument with a court page, who could not have been more than fourteen years old. The argument ended when he plunged his sword into the boy's body and killed him. It was a murder on sacred ground – the king's own castle of Saint-Germain. Eustache de Cavoye was finished.

The king's curious bond with Eustache must indeed have been strong. Whereas an ordinary man would almost certainly have been executed as a murderer, Eustache was allowed to escape with only the loss of his commission. The journal of the Guards regiment records:

> Fourth Company.
> Lieutenants.
> The Chevalier de Cavoye.
> Forced to sell [his commission] by order of the King, for an unhappy affair that occurred at Saint-Germain.

Now Eustache was a social outcast. Never again must he show his face at court. Never again would anyone ask after him. Eustache could only vanish into the underworld. His brother Louis took pity, and allowed Eustache to live with him at his house in the Rue de la Sourdière from 1666. A year later their last surviving brother Armand was killed at the Siege of Lille. Early in 1668 they moved to the Rue de Bourbon.

From this point on, Eustache effectively disappeared from public view, becoming a rather shadowy and elusive figure, and getting deeper and deeper into debt. Financially, only Louis kept him above water. In 1668 we find Louis taking legal steps to ensure that Eustache's rent be deducted from his allowance at source before he could fritter it away – for Eustache owed him an incredible £1400 in back rent. Without Louis to take the brunt of such debts, Eustache could not survive financially. Then, later that year, came an event which was to change the pattern of both men's lives. Louis de Cavoye and his bitter enemy the Marquis de Louvois simultaneously fell in love with the same married woman, one Sidonia de Courcelles: at 4 am one morning behind the Hotel de Turenne, Louis fought a duel with her husband, and both men were arrested. Louvois pressed for the death sentence for his enemy; the King, urged the other way by Colbert, preferred to be lenient to his friend. But whatever the King's feelings, Louis could not escape a brief spell in the Bastille, before being released and returning to favour in 1672.[4] Eustache was on his own.

Left alone, without a restraining influence and without his only source of financial help, Eustache must have finished his annual allowance for 1669 fairly quickly. By early summer he was probably broke again, desperate for money, and with no further income on the horizon until 1670. It is at this point that Eustache completely disappears. What did he do? What was his scheme to earn himself more money? One can only suppose that he hoped to get it from the king somehow, and enlisted the aid of his best friend Lauzun as a liaison at Court, a move which backfired when Lauzun betrayed him.

Eustache de Cavoye is undoubtedly our man. He was the right age: the prisoner who thought himself 'about 60' years old on arrival at the Bastille was in fact 61. He disappeared at the right time. He had the right name, the right religion and the right nationality. A soldier, he was indeed 'much travelled', as the Abbot Lenglet assured us was an attribute of the masked man. He has been described as large, healthy and well-built, just as the masked man was variously described by the doctor of the Bastille, by the gaoler Blainvilliers, and by the peasants of Palteau. But there is one point to which we have not referred – the mask itself, and the masked man's probable resemblance to the king. The masked man's face was hidden so that 'he would not be recognised', at a time when the king was the only instantly recognisable person in France. We do not have a picture of Eustache, but we do have a picture of his brother Louis, who presumably looked fairly similar to him. In fact, *Louis de Cavoye and King Louis* XIV *looked virtually identical*. The pair invited comparison at the time; how amazing it must have been that these two close friends should look like twin brothers. So whatever Eustache's misdemeanour, it was surely connected with the suspicious fact that he almost certainly resembled the king very closely.

Whatever Eustache was doing to earn a living by 1669, he had come down in the world so disastrously that he had already disappeared from society; it is hard to find out about his doings in these years. So only a few people would have noticed if he disappeared from existence altogether: Lauzun, who would not have been surprised, and his brother, who was in prison at the time, and who upon his release was to become the king's main adviser, and so privy to all the closest royal secrets anyway. Perhaps Eustache had even been forced to take a job as a gentleman's valet to support himself in his brother's absence? If he had, it is the sort of thing that would have appealed to Louvois' cruel nature. That may or may not be the case – nobody knows. But what we do need to discover is exactly what Eustache was really up to during this period. Remember that we are looking for a man with some skill in the use of drugs.

Perhaps we are even looking for a poisoner.

Notes on Chapter 16

1 There were two corps of musketeers: the royal musketeers and the cardinal's musketeers, between which a fierce rivalry existed.

2 François was almost completely restored to favour later when his wife faked the symptoms of a fatal illness for him, and Richelieu relented. When he realised he had been tricked, the Cardinal took it in good humour and appointed Marie to a new post, 'Superintendent of Comedy'.

3 Present was 'the eldest Cavoye, lieutenant in the Guards'. By this time only Eustache, who was the eldest surviving brother, had reached the rank of lieutenant.

4 Duels were officially illegal but socially acceptable. Louis de Cavoye's imprisonment was not an arduous one: he was allowed to sleep with his mistress every night.

17

Poison

In 1668, talk of poison was in the air. The Marquise de Brinvilliers was a sweet little lady, who had nursed her aged father through a terrible and fatal illness. She visited sick people in hospital, and was known for her good works. When her two brothers also died in agony, people felt sorry for her. When her husband developed the same symptoms, people began to be suspicious. Her lover and accomplice, fearing for his own safety should she ever tire of him, betrayed her to the police. The Marquise de Brinvilliers, it was revealed, was a fiend. She had murdered her entire family: she had visited the invalids in hospital only in order to experiment with poisons, to see which were the most agonising and the most deadly mixtures. The Marquise slipped out of the hands of the police and disappeared. But nobody discovered who had provided her with the poison.

The Marquise's murders were thought by some to be an isolated incident. Then, in 1670, came another blow: Henrietta of Orléans, sister-in-law, cousin and lover of King Louis xiv, and sister and lover to King Charles ii of England,[1] fell ill in suspicious circumstances. She too was to die in agony. It seemed likely, as she told those around her, that she had been poisoned.[2] Louis had her correspondence investigated: both kings wanted action. The police and judiciary became involved; and before long two high-ranking policemen, including the Chief of Police, Daubray, had died of poison as well. An investigating judge, Nallot, one of Louvois' aides, died in similar circumstances in 1673. It was clear that there was an organised conspiracy at work to supply and use poison. The new chief of police, La Reynie, determined to root it out.

A priest from Nôtre Dame visited La Reynie in his new office and warned that more and more people were coming to him and confessing to murder by poison. So many, in fact, that it was almost becoming a social hobby amongst the well-heeled ladies of Paris. In 1676 the Marquise de Brinvilliers was caught. She was tortured, but said nothing, except to complain – on her way to beheading – that she should be the one to have to die when so many people of quality were just as guilty as her. Still, there were no definite clues as to who lay at the centre of the web. Then, in 1679, La Reynie got his breakthrough. Acting on a tip-off, two minor poisoners, Madame Bosse and Madame Vigoureux, were arrested; in the hope of clemency they chose to talk. Between them they revealed an extraordinary world of poison and contract murders; where assassination was commonplace, and carried out not by thugs but by sweet old ladies with bottles of chemicals; where black magic prevailed over prayer and babies were kidnapped and sacrificed to Satan at the altar. A world where, as La Reynie said, 'men's lives were up for sale as a matter of everyday bargaining'. Now he could lift the lid off Parisian society.

La Reynie went straight to Louvois and the king. The three men set up a special court to deal with the case, called the Chambre Ardente. It met for the first time on 19 April 1679, and it was horrified by what it heard. First in the dock was another prisoner, La Voisin, senior accomplice of Bosse and Vigoureux, who implicated a stream of duchesses, countesses, marchionesses and even princesses in murder and sacrifice. The writer Racine was amongst those charged, and the Marshal de Luxembourg was also indicted for reasons of sexual deviancy. La Voisin even named Madame de Montespan's maid, Oeillets, who had borne a child by the King,[3] as one of her customers.

For her crimes, Madame Vigoureux was tortured to death. Bosse and La Voisin survived the torture, and were burnt alive. The trial, said the king, must go on.

Then, the whole trial was turned upside down and thrown into confusion, by an event that evaporated the determination of the king. Three black magicians were interrogated by the court, and for the first time revealed two names. One of these names will be of interest to us; the other name stopped the investigators in their tracks – that of Madame de Montespan. Montespan had usurped the position of Louise de la Vallière as royal mistress back in 1667; and in the course of the investigation into those years, the chamber heard that Montespan too had come to the poisoners for aid.

Two of the black priests gave evidence against Montespan – Lesage, the lover of La Voisin, and Guiborg, a thin, shambling, red-faced monster of 70 who had worked for her, and who was on trial for the mass murder of small children. They revealed that in 1667 and in 1668 Montespan had taken part in black masses aimed against Louise de la Vallière. They told how she had lain naked on the altar and offered herself to Satan if she could become the King's mistress, as part of a black mass involving the murder of a baby. They told also of how she had fed love potions to the King to win his favour, with apparent success; and how she had finally decided to poison him for his infidelities to her, and had bought chemicals to this end.[4]

The personal embarrassment to the king was enormous. The whole affair was also heartbreaking. He loved Montespan, and could not bear to punish her, but she was finished as royal mistress. An exorcism was said for the soul of the poor departed Louise. And the Chambre Ardente was closed down too. Nobody must hear any more. All the society figures charged with murder and other crimes escaped scot free; only the small fry were punished. La Reynie was furious, for all his work was ruined. The King even ordered him to destroy all copies of the

Chamber's records, so that nobody would ever know what had occurred. But he didn't. One copy he kept for himself at police headquarters, which is how we come to know what happened.

Before the Chamber was closed, the interrogation of the black priests was completed, and they came up with another name. A magician named Belot was brought before the Chamber, and tied to an apparatus which crushed his knees under planks, which were progressively hammered down with mallets. Under the immense pain, Belot spoke of a drug dealer who had provided the poisons, who – he said – had been a house guest at the Court of Saint Eloi. The Court of Saint Eloi was the home of the Marquise de Brinvilliers, the multiple-murderess who had fled in 1668. The drug dealer's name was d'Auger.

The proceedings of the Chamber exist in form of reported speech. Rendered into direct speech, the interrogation reads something like this:

INTERROGATOR: Who introduced you to d'Auger, the drug dealer who was staying at the Court of Saint Eloi?

BELOT: I knew him because he kept his mistress in the Rue Soly, in the house of La Chéron [another poisoner].

INTERROGATOR: You went there frequently, didn't you, with your accomplice Duval?

BELOT: I didn't. Duval often went there alone.

INTERROGATOR: Was it from d'Auger that you got the drugs you needed, or from another supplier? One of his friends?

BELOT: I never got any drugs, not from d'Auger or any other drug dealer.

INTERROGATOR: So where did you get the opium you were offering, with the black poppy that you claimed would put someone to sleep? ... What do you know of d'Auger? What business did you have together?

BELOT: Nothing! (Crying out) I know nothing!

Belot's arms, legs and ribcage were smashed before he went to the scaffold two hours later. The poisoner La Chéron, the lady who had lived with d'Auger's mistress, was burnt alive.

Belot was not the only prisoner to speak of a mysterious supplier of drugs. The priest Guiborg also came up with more sensational revelations. He astounded the Chamber by revealing that Henrietta of Orléans herself had arranged a black mass at no less a place than the royal palace. She too had lain naked on the altar and offered herself to Satan, to try and bring about the death of her husband Philippe, the king's brother.[5] This was doubly embarrassing for King Louis, whose flirtation with Henrietta was no secret. But who was the man who had arranged the ceremony, and who had hired Guiborg to say the mass?

INTERROGATOR: Who engaged you to go and say the mass at the royal palace?

GUIBORG: It was the same drug dealer for whom I said one of these masses before, in the St Victor quarter. The drug dealer was at the royal palace while I waited at de Gand's house, where the ornaments for the saying of the mass had been brought. He returned at eleven in the evening, to say that all was not well, that there were too many people there.

INTERROGATOR: In which part of the royal palace did the mass have to be said?

GUIBORG: In one of the concierges' rooms, I think, but I couldn't say which. De Gand told me that when I was in place I would be told what was wanted, what I had to do. It was at this time that this man arrived, who had referred me to de Gand. The proposition that she

> [Henrietta] wanted me to say the mass
> at the royal palace was only made
> following another mass that I had said
> at this drug dealer's house in the St
> Victor quarter. She had heard talk of
> me and came to Petit-Pierre, who came
> to find me at St Denis. This led to my
> speaking with the drug dealer, who
> lived with his brother, in Faubourg-St
> Germain, in a great street, opposite the
> great door of the Charity Hospital,
> who proposed to me that I repeat the
> same mass that I had said for him in
> the St Victor quarter . . . I cannot say
> what the drug dealer's name was, but
> he was a tall young man, and well-
> built.

We have heard descriptions of a tall, well-built young man
before. But let us be more specific. This man lived with his
brother in a great street which lay opposite the great door
of the Charity Hospital. The Charity Hospital of Paris,
founded in 1608 and demolished in 1935, was bounded by
four streets – the Rues Saint-Benoît, Saints-Pères, Jacob
and Taranne. The great door lay on the Rue des Saints-
Pères: but there was no great street opposite, indeed until
the mid-seventeenth century only orchards lay to the south
of the hospital, beyond the Rue des Saints-Pères. Guiborg
was a 70-year-old man, trying to recall the events of ten
years previously, so his inaccuracy is not surprising. But in
1640 a major new street had been built running south
across the open land from the Rue des Saints-Pères, not
directly opposite the great door (where no street was ever
built) but a hundred yards to the east, opposite it across
the fields. Today it is called the Rue de Lille. The street
names of Paris have changed frequently during the past
three centuries, but in 1670, when Henrietta died, the street
still bore its original name – the Rue de Bourbon. Eustache

d'Auger de Cavoye lived with his brother in the Rue de Bourbon.

One can only suspect that Henrietta's mysterious apothecary, the Marquise de Brinvilliers' poisoner d'Auger, and Eustache de Cavoye were one and the same. The period is right: not only must the mass at the royal palace have been heard before Henrietta's death in 1670, but Belot spoke of d'Auger's mistress living in the house of La Chéron in the Rue Soly. La Chéron moved out of the Rue Soly in 1669. The physical description also fits Eustache, as does the name and the address. And Eustache, as we know from his exploits at Roissy and his expertise with Fouquet's drugs and remedies, was involved in both black magic and pharmacy. Whether or not Eustache was really a poisoner and black magician, there was certainly a major figure called d'Auger involved in such matters in the late 1660s, who seems to have completely disappeared from view somewhere around 1669. If they were not the same man, the coincidence would be enormous.

In addition, the infamous Marquise de Brinvilliers was actually a distant relative of the Cavoyes, and she herself implicated an anonymous cousin in her schemes. She also confessed to having had an affair with him. These are all extraordinary charges: but perhaps we know now what Eustache de Cavoye was doing in those shadowy years, and what kind of person he really was – certainly not the sort to engender much sympathy. But poisoners and black magicians do not have their faces masked and are not kept in high security and comfort, even if they are known to the king and resemble him closely. The secret of the man in the iron mask has yet to be discovered. But perhaps we have discovered, in the flight of the Marquise de Brinvilliers, the loss of another of Eustache's protectors, another reason why he might need money. Perhaps we have also discovered, in his past lifestyle and in his presumably abortive efforts to obtain that extra money, the reasons that he showed no great regret or desire to escape his comfortable prison. We have certainly discovered, in his character, the reasons why his family and friends were ready to disown him so easily and why such a man would not be missed.

The reaction of Louis de Cavoye to the imprisonment of his brother is understandable. What else could he do but acquiesce? He had become the king's closest confidant; he had a lot to lose. He was Grand Marshal of the Royal Household, and he mixed with famous men like Racine and Boileau. He was known as one of the most handsomely built, best-dressed men at court, as a skilful duellist, as 'Brave Cavoye'. He was described in contemporary records as 'a fine looking man' (his brothers were said to be 'even finer by all accounts'). His military exploits, including the crossing of the Rhine, were well-publicised. The diarist St Simon wrote of him:

> At all courts there are remarkable people who, without talent, without distinguished birth, and without influential friends, achieve familiarity with the elite, and finally, no-one knows how, become a power to be reckoned with. Such a man was Cavoye.

Quite apart from the enormous saving that Louis de Cavoye would have made when Eustache disappeared, taking all his debts with him, and the embarrassment that he would now be spared, we know from elsewhere that Louis was not afraid to compromise his principles in return for advancement. For instance, part of his promotion had involved marrying the immensely ugly Mademoiselle de Coëtlogon, the queen's maid of honour, a task he fell to without showing a flicker of dissent. The king had been kind to him: not only had he allowed the company of his mistress every night of his gaol sentence, but he had been made a Marquis soon after his release. Now was the time to show his gratitude. Louis de Cavoye died in 1715, the same year as his king; his will made it clear that he was the only surviving Cavoye brother. He knew that Eustache was dead.

But what of the rest of his family? Louis may not have cared, but Eustache had more than one sister. Maybe a sister's compassion is greater than that of a brother, because in 1678 one of the Cavoye sisters started to ask awkward questions about what had become of Eustache. Where was her brother? In answer to her enquiries she received this letter, sent from the prison at St Lazare, in June 1678:

My dear Sister,

If you knew what I am suffering I have no doubts that you would make the utmost efforts to save me from the cruel persecution and captivity where I have been detained for more than ten years by the tyranny of my brother Monsieur de Cavoye, under false pretexts, in order to kill me, to enrage me, and so that he could enjoy our property more freely; he had the intention of taking me away and then depriving me of my freedom, which was the only thing I had left to enjoy after the donation to him that he had forced me to make by surprise.[6]

I beg you my dear sister, for the love of Jesus Christ, not to abandon me in my current state; you must act principally for the safety of my soul, because I will never confess while I remain here, not being able to forget the cruel treatment that I receive every day from the most ungrateful of all men . . . Let yourself be moved, my dear sister, by the prayers of a poor wretch, who leads a languishing life which will finish soon if you do not have a pity for him. If you refuse me this mercy, then you will have to account for the salvation of my soul before God, and you will incur his very great displeasure for not having helped a brother who can have no help in the world but you.

If you have the goodness as to accord me your assistance, then I beg you to take all the action that you judge necessary for my liberty and for my affairs as regards the King. In receiving this grace I am indebted to you with all my heart.

Eustache

A flurry of information about Eustache suddenly surfaced over the next few months. Another petition was addressed to the King:

> Sire, Cavoye who has been detained under a royal warrant in the prison of Saint-Lazare for eleven-and-a-half years implores Your Majesty most humbly to do him the grace of hearing his just complaints against the Lord of Cavoye, his brother . . . If your majesty does not wish to look into the matter himself, I implore you most humbly to refer me to the heads of my family, so that they might decide whether I deserve such cruel treatment . . . I am scarcely furnished with the necessities of life, and I am denied those comforts which might reduce the sorrow and the pain which I have borne so long, and which have weakened my health and exhausted my spirit to the extent that I have barely any more strength.

On August 17th, 1678, the register of the King's orders shows the instruction to the Governor of St Lazare that 'M. De Cavoye should have communication with no-one at all, not even with his sister'. Then, soon afterwards, Eustache officially dies. The Count of Brienne, at Saint-Lazare, writes an obituary:

> 'Here in this coffin at Saint-Lazare lies
> Cavoye, whose saint's name was Eustache
> An intransigent gent overcome by drink
> And death, which took him by surprise'.

On the face of it these documents would seem to dash the whole case. They fly in the face of all the evidence so far. But in fact they do contain a number of ambiguities; mistakes, for instance, that the real Eustache would never have made.

First, as part of a search to discover the identity of the man in the iron mask, the French author Julius Topin made a study of every state prisoner incarcerated in France between 1660 and 1710. There was no sign of any Eustache

Dauger at St Lazare prison. There was no trial, no sentenc-
ing, no committal and no correspondence about any
Dauger at all. Secondly, and more importantly, 'Eustache'
complains that he has been imprisoned by his brother
Louis so that Louis can take control of the family property.
But we know that when Louis de Cavoye had been gaoled
in the Bastille for fighting an illegal duel in 1668, Eustache
was still at liberty. The first letter sets the date of Eustache's
imprisonment at 1668, the second letter at 1667, when
Eustache and Louis had not even moved to the Rue de
Bourbon. Even if Louis de Cavoye was now important
enough to obtain a royal warrant to imprison his brother
so easily (a doubtful point), the dates do not fit. And where
is this warrant? Why is it not in the records?

There are other inconsistencies. Why had 'Eustache'
waited ten years to protest? Why the sudden flurry of letters
after a decade of inactivity, followed by a protestation of ill
health and then a convenient death? Why should a mere
drunk be denied all communication with his relatives? And
why should 'Eustache' ask to be judged by the heads of his
family, when the real Eustache would know that there were
no 'heads of his family'? He *was* the head of his family, at
least until his brother Louis had taken over, and it was his
brother Louis that 'Eustache' was supposedly appealing
against. Why did this 'Eustache' talk of his brother enjoying
their joint property? The real Eustache would know that
his mother had officially disinherited him of all family
property in her will. Furthermore, he had even signed a
document confirming to his brother that he relinquished all
rights in the matter. The real Eustache Dauger de Cavoye
simply wouldn't have made such mistakes. To say the least,
the documents are suspicious.

The ingenuity would seem to lie in directing Eustache's
sister to her brother Louis as the man responsible. Louis
was the one man she would trust and obey, the head of her
own family: but for all that, a man who would deceive her
at the King's bidding. And if the involvement of her brother
Louis were not enough for her, the involvement of the King

was a very dangerous area to be getting into. Nobody ever interfered with the King's affairs. Neither is the tone of 'Eustache's' appeal to his sister very pleasant – whingeing, and threatening. As far as the authorities were concerned, it did the trick. Nothing more was heard about the missing Eustache. Except, of course, 400 miles away at Pignerol . . .

It may seem extravagant to dismiss these documents as forgeries. But the fact remains that they do contradict other factual evidence. Somebody is lying. And who had better reason to lie than an administration which had consistently shown that it had something very important indeed to hide? We have seen already that official records of the case had been liberally tampered with.

For the rest of them, the Cavoye family kept conspicuously silent about the errant Eustache both before and after his arrest. Despite the shame that he had brought upon them, it seems a slightly suspicious silence. As we know, benefits were heaped upon Louis de Cavoye, the chosen head of the family, to the point of becoming a marquis. St Simon's remark that his success came 'without talent, distinguished birth or influence' must be considered slightly suspicious. But what is less well known is that the crown paid out a pension of £6000, equivalent to ten times that amount now, to his mother Marie. François de Cavoye, her husband, had been a fine Captain of Musketeers and servant to both Richelieu and the King; but the scale of the award implies that Marie was being rewarded for something more than gallantry on the part of her husband – she was being paid for discretion.[7] Military pensions were not normally given at all, let alone such large ones. So whatever secret it was that Eustache had learnt or simply abused for his own benefit, it seems to have been a Cavoye family secret as well as a secret of the royal house of France.

At the centre of the whole conspiracy to silence Eustache lay the King of France, Louis XIV. At the root of this whole mystery lie his secrets and his decisions. Louis it was who paid out fabulous sums to the Cavoyes, to gaolers and to family friends to ensure their silence, and to keep the

masked man in comfort: Louis it was who was equally
prepared to kill to preserve his secrets, in this case a secret
that might hurt his descendants a hundred years later. If
Louis' behaviour can be explained, then the clues will be
complete: and from the final clues must come the solution.

Notes on Chapter 17

1 A confusing piece of genealogy. Louis XIII's sister, Henrietta,
married Charles I of England. Louis XIII went on to bear two sons,
Louis XIV and Philippe of Orléans. Amongst others, Charles I
bore Charles II, James II and another Henrietta, who then married
Philippe, and became Henrietta of Orléans. See Appendix B.

2 She cried out: 'If I were not a Christian I would kill myself, so
dreadful are my pains.' In London, furious crowds attacked
Frenchmen in the streets, and threatened ambassador Colbert.

3 Louis XIV was obviously an impatient lover. When Madame de
Montespan kept him waiting for too long outside her bedchamber,
he was wont to have his way with her maid on the couch outside,
instead.

4 At which point the king began to understand why he had been
suffering bouts of ferocious headaches recently.

5 The reason seems to have been that Philippe was an outrageous
homosexual. As the king's younger brother, he had been brought
up as a girl, to quell any thoughts he might have had of usurping
the position of the king; obviously it was an upbringing that had
a lasting effect on him.

6 A reference to the £1,400 owed by Eustache to Louis, that Louis
took legal steps to recover in 1668.

7 Scarron said that she was one of a small minority of people so
influential as to be respected as much as princesses.

18

A gift of God

'Beyond all doubt, my ruling passion is the pursuit of glory.'

The words of King Louis XIV, aptly summing up his seventy-two-year reign over France. Louis XIV turned the French monarchy into a public spectacle, far more than do the monarchies of today; but the power and the glory that the public were invited to behold were anything but illusory. Behind all the fêtes, the parties, the palaces and the riches that he put on display, Louis concentrated more power into his hands than had been seen for many years in France. And he was prepared to use that power, with great cruelty if necessary, to reinforce his vainglory.

It was not always so. As a child, growing up in turbulent times under the protection of his mother Queen Anne and of Cardinal Mazarin, he was – as the historian J. B. Wolf tells us – 'reserved and sober'. He was content to enjoy the company of his young friends and the material benefits of kingship without interfering with Mazarin's business of running the country, just as King Louis XIII before him had never really troubled his own prime minister, Cardinal Richelieu. But around the time of Mazarin's death, in March 1661, a radical change overcame the 22-year-old King: a change that startled observers. The young man who everyone had expected would stay in the back seat suddenly developed an obsessive taste for power at the expense of those around him, and a liking for the glories and splendours that royalty could bring. It was almost as if something had happened to change his perspective on life: as if he had learnt something that made him determined to act more like a true king.

On the morrow of Mazarin's death, 10 March 1661, Louis called together all the chief ministers of the country in order to make the following statement. 'The time has come', he said, 'for me to govern myself . . . from now on, I forbid you to sign the smallest act without my permission.' Louis announced that he had decided to become a good king and to learn everything there was to know about kingship. Nobody believed him. For the son of the indolent Louis XIII, it was an extraordinary statement. As Voltaire said, 'Women with any pretence of beauty flattered themselves that they would rule a prince of 22.' But when Nicolas Fouquet – who despite the king's declaration still confidently expected to assume the reins of government – was swept aside so magisterially by the young Louis, everybody realised that he was in earnest. It was not a pleasant realisation.

It was not just that Louis assumed full political power. His behaviour began to verge upon the megalomaniacal. He immediately abolished all acts of Parliament and grants of nobility made over the previous thirty years. In 1665 he sentenced 349 provincial nobles to death for minor financial irregularities. Others suffered for his prestige. He took to describing himself as 'The Emperor', and ordered that all foreign ships should salute passing French ships at sea (except for the English navy, which was a little too strong to push around). When the Genoese refused, he had the town of Genoa shelled by over a thousand cannon, with serious loss of life. And he even went so far as to threaten the pope.

Life could be just as inconvenient at home. Louis revoked religious freedoms and unleashed savage persecutions on over 200,000 Protestants, carried out by the pitiless and brutal Louvois: their treatment was so appalling that even the pope complained to Paris. Louis also took control of the police and the courts, forcing them to carry out his demands, and imposing crippling taxes upon the people in order to finance his revels. Those who defaulted on their tax payments had soldiers forcibly billeted upon their houses. Life in France, according to the Venetian ambassador, was tantamount to 'slavery'.

At the opposite end of the scale, life at court was one enormous circus; at the centre of it all, the 'Sun King' turned his own daily life into a spectator sport. His every move was watched by large gatherings of hushed and fawning courtiers. Everybody had to observe his fashions and copy them, such as the long, curly wigs that everyone had to wear when the king started to go bald. For anyone to take leave of absence from the simple joy of beholding the king was social death; but around his person orchestras played, great feasts were consumed, plays were performed, and courtiers gambled with pieces of gold, which made life that much more bearable.

Louis altered the times of the royal meals. Breakfast moved from 7 am to midday, lunch moved to 5 pm and dinner to midnight. A typical lunch for Louis consisted of four bowls of soup, a whole chicken stuffed with truffles, a large plate of salad, followed by a plate of mutton, then ham, then a dish of pastry, then fresh fruit and preserves to finish. His sexual appetites could be just as lavish. He spurned the queen, and took three lovers, Louise de la Vallière, Madame de Montespan and Madame de Maintenon, on whom he lavished huge diamonds and pearls, and power to match. But around, in between and during his infatuations with those women were scores of others, such as Marie Angélique de Fontanges, whom he described as being 'as beautiful as an angel . . . but devastatingly stupid'. Louis could afford to take his pick of the women at court whenever he felt like it, and no-one is really sure how many bastards he sired.

The setting for all this luxury, the palace of Versailles, was personally commissioned by Louis to be the most magnificent residence in history. It took 20,000 workers ten years to build; hundreds of them died in the process. Every face on every fresco, every carving and each one of the many statues of gods at the palace were the same – that of Louis XIV. Young courtiers were sent out from Versailles to do battle in the king's name. All over Europe, soldiers fought to win more territory to add to the royal glory. Generation after generation of *jeunesse dorée* – whole families like the Cavoyes – were slaughtered at Louis' bidding. Huge areas were devastated by his troops. By the time of his death in 1715, over a million Frenchmen had died to feed Louis XIV's lust for fame and power.

There must have been a point to all this, a reason for this rapid personality change. Louis had become obsessed with his image as a king. He vainly wanted to raise his own kingship to the status of the semi-divine in the eyes of posterity. All the descriptions that we have today of what a great and good man this glorious monarch was were written only because their authors were expected to do so in return for their keep. In fact the accolades might as well have been commissioned directly by Louis, for all that they really tell us about him. St Simon, who had a great respect for royalty in general, wrote after his death: 'Praise – or, to be honest, flattery – pleased him to such a point that the grossest were well received, and more base examples still better enjoyed.'

The result is that today, despite clear evidence to the contrary, Louis is sometimes thought of as a decent monarch. In this respect, he succeeded in his public relations exercise. And yet he was capable of extraordinary cruelty. When a party of courtiers, including the young Lauzun, got lost on a hunting trip in the forest and darkness fell, they were lucky enough to find a house in the woods; the owner, Fargues, took them in and gave them shelter and abundant hospitality, possibly saving their lives. On their returning to court and singing Fargues' praises to the king, Louis recognised the name of a man who had once been involved in political unrest but had been completely pardoned by the courts and had retired to the country. Never

one to forget an old adversary, Louis elicited the whereabouts of the house and sent his agents to seize Fargues,
who was then brought back to court and beheaded.

But if some later historians were fooled by Louis' battery
of official praise, contemporaries seem to have been discreetly astonished by what kind of man Louis had become.
Much was made at the time of the king's extraordinarily
inflated attempts at self-aggrandisement. Nobody expected
it to happen, and when it did they were bemused. Marcel
Pagnol has summed up contemporary reaction to Louis'
behaviour: 'it was as if this vanity was not part of the
personality and of the character of the king'. Historians
have generally put forward a rather unconvincing case that
this was a character trait that suddenly bloomed from
nowhere. According to John Letts for instance, 'his taste
for outrageous magnificence [was] no doubt always latent'.
In fact, this abrupt personality change seems more like a
conscious attempt to prove a specific point to the world.

Combined with this catalogue of self-promotion was a
marked royal insecurity that also bears investigation. Louis
was obsessed with the legality and respectability of everything he did, and employed several jurists to put a legal
face on his more dubious enterprises. He trusted nobody.
His personal bodyguard was Swiss, not French. He
employed networks of paid informers to spy on his courtiers. All private mail was liable to be intercepted and read.
He confined all his secrets to a tiny group of ministers, who
had few social connections at court and who were always
succeeded by their sons, so as to keep everything 'in the
family'. All of them owed their success entirely to him. But
he also set these ministers against each other, let none of
them take decisions without his permission, and removed
them without compunction when they ceased to please.
Further to the mysterious ends of Louvois and Barbezieux
came the treatment of Colbert: when he died in disgrace in
1683, the king even tried to damage his coffin during the
funeral. And then of course there was the fanatical attention

that he devoted to his one masked captive, and the obsessive security surrounding the masked man's imprisonment. Every day Louis took three hours away from his entertainments to closet himself with one or other of his ministers, discussing the affairs of state: we know from the letters of Louvois and the king that the masked prisoner must have been discussed at many of these sessions.

Why was Louis so unsure about his position and so determined to show off his own royalty? These were the actions of an insecure man, a man worried about something. I would venture to suggest that they show themselves to be the actions of a man who was worried about the legality of his own position. We know there is a strong possibility that the masked man's secret was a dynastic secret; the behaviour of Louis XIV, at the same time concentrating and demonstrating power, with one eye on posterity and one eye on some unspecified internal secret that could bring his whole monarchy down, suggests that the King of France was trying to cover up some irregularity in his own royal credentials. This may seem a sweeping statement to make, on the basis of his authoritarian leanings and his outrageous social tendencies; but there is a lot more to his insecurity than that. For the answer to this dynastic mystery, it is necessary to go back to the early part of the seventeenth century, and the curious circumstances surrounding the birth of Louis XIV.

At the time we find Louis XIII on the throne, an insubstantial king who had virtually handed control of the country over to Cardinal Richelieu. Richelieu became the king's inseparable friend, confessor and protector. Others who tried to gain influence or authority ended up in exile or on the scaffold. Supported by his musketeers, Richelieu concentrated power about himself and his central government, destroying the power of the old high-ranking nobles and replacing them with ministers from bourgeois professional families elevated to the peerage. But there was a fly in the ointment: for King Louis XIII was a man uninterested in sex, love and women in general, and there was no prospect whatsoever of an heir to the throne being produced. Waiting in the wings was Gaston of Orléans, the king's hated brother, first in line to the throne, and head of the group of nobles who opposed Richelieu and all he stood for.

'I avoid love,' said Louis XIII categorically at the time. 'His affections were purely spiritual', commented a contemporary, 'and his enjoyments always chaste.' The one thing that Louis XIII disliked more than sex was Spaniards; and in 1615, for political reasons, he was forced to marry Anne, the daughter of the King of Spain, confusingly named Anne of Austria. It was not a recipe for domestic bliss. The royal couple detested the sight of each other, and it took Richelieu four years to persuade the king to try to consummate the marriage. The king and queen spent one uncomfortable night together, and it was later claimed (without any proof) that the queen had miscarried. Other reconciliations were tried, but with no effect. When the queen definitely did miscarry in 1631, she had been trying to keep the pregnancy secret, which hardly suggests the King had anything to do with it. The couple stayed literally miles away from each other, and no child was born. Their dislike was deep, lasting and mutual.

In 1630 Louis nearly died, an episode which brought home to all concerned the real possibility that Gaston might take over the throne. Nobody wanted that, certainly not Louis, who had already suffered attempts by his brother to unseat him, and least of all Richelieu, who knew that if Gaston became king it would certainly lead to his own death. Gaston had already tried to have him murdered. Richelieu's deputy Mazarin, too, would have been in great personal danger if Gaston took charge, as would all the ministers. Queen Anne would have lost all influence. Yet the royal couple simply could not produce an heir, and both were growing older. The fault seemed to be the king's. The queen was not short of male admirers; but he was colourless, always ill, unattractive and uninterested. He suffered from a wasting disease which seems to have made him impotent. But then, early in December 1637, after twenty-two years of barren marriage, came a curious event. Louis XIII went travelling with Cardinal Richelieu and François de Cavoye. A few weeks later he made a public announcement that he was commending the provision of a son and heir to the Virgin Mary: it was almost as if he acknowledged that the matter was now out of his hands. Nine months later, the Queen gave birth to the future Louis XIV.

Everybody knows the implications of the Virgin birth, and how Joseph, the 'father', did not actually participate. Louis XIII asked his people to believe that a similar religious miracle had taken place. Said Richelieu: 'Never has there been such rejoicing as for this new favour that Heaven has granted to the Kingdom of France'. But perhaps there was more to it than that. Perhaps the king had a sense of irony too, and was trying to imply that he too had not participated in the pregnancy. For the official story of the conception of Louis XIV was unbelievable, to say the least. It went as follows: King Louis XIII was on his way to Versailles, which at that time was a small royal hunting lodge, when a fearful storm forced him and his entourage to take shelter. Quite by chance, they were passing the Louvre at the time, where quite by chance the queen was in residence. The only bedroom prepared was the queen's, so the royal couple slept together, and lo and behold conceived a son. The date for this episode was said to have been 5 December 1637, exactly nine months to the day before Louis XIV's birth.

A story like this had to be published, for it was common public knowledge that under normal circumstances nothing would induce the king and queen to share a bed. But this tale is rather preposterous. Apart from the suspiciously exact date, there were several places near the Louvre in Paris where the king could stay, and hundreds of rooms in the Louvre where he could take shelter. It is asking a lot to believe that the king of France could not have had a separate bed made up for himself. In what can only be interpreted as a further irony, the child was officially named

'Louis Dieudonné'. Literally, it means 'The gift of God'. In more common parlance, it was a name often applied sarcastically to those whose fathers were unknown.

The child's birth at least was above board. Crowds of people were allowed to come in and watch the royal delivery take place. The Princess of Condé, the Duchess of Vendôme and the Countess of Soissons were officially appointed to witness the birth to ensure that no trickery took place. So important was the survival of the child that special orders were given to the royal doctors that he must pull through 'whatever happens', even if it meant the queen's life. In fact it was a successful, problem-free birth, and a handsome, plump and healthy baby was presented, to the cheers of the crowd, at eleven o'clock that morning. In what could have proved to be a dangerous move, he was even handed to a stunned Gaston of Orléans to verify that he was indeed a boy. Fortunately, Gaston didn't drop him, and was later seen returning to his estate in tears.

There were, however, public suspicions about his parenthood. Official attempts were made to stamp out this seditious talk: careful censorship made sure that such suspicions were not easily voiced. But they were certainly held. Racine wrote ambiguously about Louis XIV:

His birth however obscure,
his race unknown,
The world in him
its sovereign Chief would own.

But if such doubts were justified nobody minded much, for France had a new heir instead of the unpopular Gaston. After Charles I was executed by the English revolutionaries in 1649, the Parisian mob forced its way into the royal palace and filed through the child's room all night long, not to take similar action against the young King but to check that he was safe in bed. Louis XIII, by contrast, took little interest in his son, and retreated to his former pleasures, although he did once complain: 'I am dissatisfied with my son ... when he saw me he cried as if he had seen the devil.'

A second son, Philippe, was born in 1640, but there was no need to explain his parenthood so elaborately. The novelty had worn off. Philippe was only there as an insurance policy against any illness which might befall his elder brother. With the succession secured, Cardinal Richelieu died on 4 December 1642, disease finally carried off Louis XIII in the Spring of 1643,[1] and when Gaston finally died as well Philippe took over the title of Orléans. The new King Louis, succeeding to the throne at the age of five, was placed officially under the regency of Queen Anne; but in practice he fell mainly under the guiding influence of his godfather, the new prime minister Cardinal Mazarin, who became his mother's lover into the bargain. He was a voracious child. His mother could not cope with his demand for milk, and he went through eight wet nurses. The royal surgeon, Dionis, commented: 'When they did not have enough milk to satisfy him, he would bite their teats.' Unusually, he had been born with teeth.

As the boy grew up, it soon became clear that he was nothing like his supposed father. He was a healthy young man with a voracious appetite. He was both athletic and elegant, and could dance, hunt and ride with equal facility. He was possessed with a natural grace and a marvellous physique. Like his father, he was forced into a political marriage, with the Spanish Princess Marie-Thérèse in 1660. But unlike his father, he was to prove fertile both within and outside his marriage.

One of Louis XIV's biographers, J. B. Wolf, reflects the confusion surrounding the differences between the two:

Everyone agreed that [Louis XIV] was a beautiful child and that he was extraordinarily robust; good health and physical beauty were to be characteristic of this prince ... and the fact that he was to live seventy-seven years testified to his physical toughness. Geneticists speak of hybrid vigour that results from the crossing of strains that have long been separated; something like this may have happened in the case of Louis de Dieudonné . . . his father looked more like the Medicis, but Louis XIV seems to have inherited the physical make-up of his Burgundian ancestors.

The young king never talked about Louis XIII, never honoured his father's memory, and never wanted to hear about him. His devotion to his mother and Mazarin, on the other hand, was complete. He seems to have been at least a pleasant young man. But after his coming of age, and after the death of Mazarin, came the transition to pompous, spectacular, brutal and secretive absolute monarchy. Despite the reliance he put on his few closest ministers, Lionne, Colbert, Le Tellier and then Louvois, he never really trusted anybody again. What had he learnt that changed his attitude so? Could it be that his mother had told him the truth about his conception and his birth? What was the truth?

For her part, there is a suggestion that Queen Anne also underwent a personality change. After the birth of her children, the playful, frivolous, flirtatious soul who had charmed the court became a religious lady more inclined to worship and prayer: 'a pious Queen who spent hours every day praying to God'.[2] It was too late to be the result of the birth of Louis XIV, but too early to be connected with the death of her husband and the chaos that followed; nobody could see a reason, unless it was connected with her reaching the age of forty! So what might have happened to depress Queen Anne around the time of her fortieth birthday, in 1641?

The son she had borne, Louis XIV, who was so unlike his supposed father, lived until 1 September 1715, four days short of his seventy-seventh birthday. Early in August he had been seized by violent pains in his leg, and everybody knew that the end must be near, but the king continued to rule from his deathbed. His heir was another five-year old, his great-grandson Louis; for he had lost his son with smallpox in 1711, and his grandson with German measles in 1712. In such circumstances there was to be another regency, and Louis bypassed his dead brother's son, also called Philippe of Orléans, in favour of the Duke of Maine, his illegitimate son by his beloved Madame de Montespan. But the day before he died, he had something to say to Philippe. He summoned his nephew into his bedchamber, sent out all the physicians, attendants and courtiers, and conversed with Philippe for some time in hushed tones behind closed doors. We can guess the nature of the secret that the King passed on.

Then Louis took confession. His last words were:

> I have made my confession to the best of my ability. My confessor has told me that I ought to put great trust in God's mercy . . . but I shall never console myself for having offended him.

I wonder if Louis told his confessor absolutely everything.

In the early hours of the first of September, the king went into a coma, and at 8.15 that morning he died. A macabre frenzy gripped France as the country erupted in delight, hoping against hope that the years of oppression were over. Parliament, overruling the dead king's wishes, threw out the Duke of Maine and installed Philippe of Orléans as regent for the young Louis xv. And as the funeral procession made its way to the cemetery of St Denis, the descendants of the same concerned Parisian crowd that had filed into the king's bedroom as a child now lined the route, shouting insults and hurling handfuls of mud and stones at the coffin.

Notes on Chapter 18

1 On 16 May 1643, having fallen into a coma, the King leapt up, pointed into space and shouted, 'Don't you see the Duke of Enghien fighting the Spaniards? Good God, how bravely he charges! They're all beaten, dead or prisoners!' With those words, he fell back on his pillow.
2 J. B. Wolf. He also commented that 'she had outgrown much of the frivolous behaviour that had characterised her early life'.

19

Criminal without a crime

On the basis of the evidence presented here, you may already have made up your own mind about the identity of the masked man. Or you may have decided, as far back as chapter 6, that he was an illegitimate black 88-year-old Swedish schoolboy, imprisoned solely to confuse the amateur detectives of a later age. On the other hand, if those possibilities offered by the French government at the time did not in your estimation strike the required note of realism, and you have not as yet formed your own opinion, then it is time to decide once and for all, on the basis of the evidence assembled in the previous chapters, just who he was and what he was punished for.

In the last few years, since the first edition of this book was published, a new theory about the masked man has gained ground: that the prisoner had no importance at all, and that his entire career was deliberately created by St Mars to boost the gaoler's own importance. A BBC-TV 'Timewatch' documentary transmitted in 1988, presented by Henry Lincoln and produced by Jonathan Dent, made it clear that 'Voltaire is the man responsible for the creation of the iron mask legend'. The programme stressed the divergence between the iron mask of Voltaire and the velvet mask of Du Jonca. 'The difference is crucial. Voltaire was creating a myth. To his reading public, an iron mask was an instrument of torture ... the idea was gruesomely titillating. On the other hand the reality, a velvet mask, was no more than a concealment.' Neither, implied the programme, was it nearly as important as a metal mask would have been.

In fact the 'Timewatch' documentary became quite high-handed about historians taking such myth-making seriously. Some scholars, it claimed, 'have even ignored evidence already in the record in order to present their own favoured theory. Nothing can be proved', concluded the programme. Well obviously, nothing can be proved out-right, or there would be no mystery. But sadly for Dent, genuine contemporary evidence of a metal mask did finally turn up, some weeks before his programme was transmit-ted. A letter was discovered that had been written by Louis Fouquet, the Bishop of Agde and a relative of Nicolas Fouquet, on September the 4th, 1687.

'Monsieur de St Mars has, by order of the King, trans-ported a state prisoner to the Isles of Sainte-Marguerite. No-one knows who he is: it is forbidden to speak his name, and he is to be killed if he should speak it himself . . . (during the journey) he was enclosed in a sedan-chair with a steel mask on his face, and all that could be learnt from St Mars was that this prisoner had been at Pignerol for many years, and that all the people believed to be dead are not necessarily so.'

So Voltaire was right after all – there was a steel mask, at least in 1687. Jonathan Dent chose, perhaps for reasons of time or money, not to do a hasty remake of his programme. Although one feels it would have been honourable to remove the phrase 'some (scholars) have even ignored evidence already in the record in order to present their own favoured theory'.

Soon afterwards, another piece of contemporary evidence was discovered, confirming that the man in the mask really was an important royal prisoner, and not a myth built up by later historians. The Abbot Mauvans, journeying to Genoa in 1687, stopped off at St Marguerite when St Mars was still on his way from Exiles with the sedan chair. He wrote that St Mars

> 'had left some time before, to go and collect that unknown prisoner, who is being transported with such great precautions, and who has been given to understand that when he is sick of living he only has to speak out his name, because the order is to give him a bullet in the head if he does. We were told that the lodging to be built for this prisoner would be connected to the governor's lodgings: that only the governor would see him, that he would serve his meals and be almost his only gaoler and guard'.

This letter was published by John Noone (a French-based Englishman whose ideas had been influential in the making of the BBC-TV documentary) in his 1988 book 'The Man Behind The Mask'. Despite the fact that Mauvans had not even met St Mars, Noone still clung to the idea that St Mars was marching about Southern France, exaggerating the importance of his prisoner in order to make himself feel important. This time the theory was presented with a novel twist, however. Instead of the *lack* of contemporary evidence proving that the masked prisoner was not really important, this time the *discovery* of a reference to a steel mask, after so many centuries of uncertainty, was held up as proof. The masked man, says Noone, was 'a well publicised sensation!' The very existence of the new letters proved that St Mars himself was creating all the fuss.

This extraordinary theory does not take a great deal of effort to demolish. It ignores the fact that the King put Dauger in Pignerol with Fouquet, previously the most important prisoner in France. It ignores the fact that he was forbidden to speak with Lauzun, again by order of the King, and that Lauzun had been promoted on the same day that Dauger's arrest warrant was issued. It ignores the fact that Louvois kept certain instructions secret from his own civil servants. It assumes that every prison guard who ever passed on their recollections was lying to create a sensation. It ignores the enormous sums authorised by Paris for the building of Dauger's special cells, and the huge salary given to St Mars (presumably as a reward for his efficiency) and the promotions the gaoler received, culminating in the ultimate accolade – the governorship of the Bastille itself. It skates over Barbezieux's express instruction that the prisoner must not be recognised. In short, it ignores the facts.

Noone would like us to believe the fantastic suggestion that Louvois and the King were unable to see through St Mars' deception because they thought their No. 1 gaoler was 'expressing himself badly'. A more meticulous man than St Mars it would be hard to envisage! In favour of his argument, Noone presents the analysis of Louvois' documents by a French investigator, Bernard Caire, who recently claimed that for three centuries everybody has been misreading the masked man's name: it is not 'Dauger' but 'Danger'. Hence, he was a nobody. One glance at Dauger's arrest warrant on page 102 is enough to show how silly this line of investigation is. The 'U' in 'Dauger' is identical to the 'U' in 'Eustache' (on line 4).

No, what does shine clearly out of the latest discoveries is that the man in the iron mask was indeed a state prisoner of tremendous importance, imprisoned in a metal mask for at least part of his prison life. Who was he? If the newly-discovered remark of St Mars is to be believed, we must bear in mind that 'all the people believed to be dead are not necessarily so.' It is a remark that could easily refer to Eustache Dauger, or to many others for that matter.

It is time now to recap, and reach a conclusion. Originally, this investigation set out to discover the identity, the secret and the reason for imprisoning 'the man in the iron mask', a royal captive of seventeenth-century France. He had been extremely well-guarded – forbidden to speak, forbidden to be seen and forbidden to have any contact with the outside world, guarded by one faithful gaoler and a host of extravagant security measures, for thirty-four

years. In fact so grotesque and stringent were these measures – coupled with the comfort and respect that he was
shown and the complete lack of any notable or likely
persons reported missing at the time – that the security
eventually defeated its own purpose, by causing far more
public interest in the case than, say, a simple incarceration
in a lunatic asylum would have done.

On the basis of this interest aroused by the masked man,
a number of things soon become apparent – that he was a
French, Catholic, well-built, well-educated and much-
travelled man of about 30, who had been imprisoned in
1669 in the castle of Pignerol, and who had died in the
Bastille in 1703. He had been buried under a false name,
his corpse had been desecrated and his belongings
destroyed. And throughout his prison life, lasting a third of
a century, he had received the close and persistent attention
of the king and his ministers. This description, it became
clear, fitted only one prisoner – Eustache Dauger, the
betrayed fugitive who had fallen into a royal trap at
Dunkirk. And Eustache Dauger, it emerged, was almost
certainly Eustache d'Auger de Cavoye, a bankrupt and
disgraced nobleman who despite the influence of his family
had dropped out of a ready-made glittering career into a
seedy world of drugs and black magic. For the story of
Eustache and the Cavoye family to have any importance in
this case – as indeed it should – one can only assume that
Eustache is our man. No plausible alternatives exist; if the
man in the iron mask had nothing to do with Eustache
Dauger, then the mystery of Eustache Dauger – why he
was arrested and what happened to him – undoubtedly
adds up to a much greater mystery than that of the masked
man himself.

The only other candidate ever seriously advanced by
historians – the Italian diplomat Mattioli – can be dismissed virtually out of hand. His arrest and crime were
widely known, there would have been no point in masking
him, he was arrested ten years too late, his name was

always used openly in official correspondence, his nationality was wrong, he definitely did not go with St Mars to Exiles, he was maltreated in prison, he had no connection with Lauzun, Fouquet or La Rivière, and there is strong evidence to suggest that he died on Sainte-Marguerite in 1694. If anything, La Rivière is a better alternative candidate. But neither would there have been any point in masking d'Auger's unfortunate companion, who also came too late and unwittingly into the plot, and almost certainly died of dropsy at Exiles. Undoubtedly, d'Auger is our man.

The identity of our criminal is firmly established. But as yet we do not know what his crime was, or his secret, for the two must surely have been linked. Before filling in the rest of the picture, on the basis of what secrets Eustache could or would have known, or what he might have done to get himself into such a predicament, one must also bear in mind the other influences at work on this story. There is Louis XIV, whose sudden extravagances contrasted so violently with his secret, obsessive fear of the masked man; Richelieu and Mazarin, the two cardinals, always at work behind the scenes to advance their own interests; the Cavoye family, so successful in all other respects, and its readiness to disown its ill-behaved son; the outrageous Count of Lauzun, that brash adventurer, whose ups and downs are inextricably woven into the story of his best friend Eustache; and Fouquet, the political casualty, who was already in possession of the facts when Eustache joined him in prison.

One must also take account of all the royal cover-ups. One must not only ask why the cover-up was needed, but what form did it take? What exactly did the authorities want us to believe? Ignoring the silly stories dreamt up to fill the heads of frivolous enquirers, the best cover-up tales were always those that distorted the truth slightly and were not too far removed from reality. Note, for instance, the plausible story of 'Marchioly', the prisoner who was 'a subject of the Duke of Mantua'. How clever would any investigator think himself who could see through this, and discover Mattioli the diplomat! Yet the most common stories about the masked man wrote him off as one of the queen's illegitimate children. We know that this is not the case, but on the other hand the truth might well lie somewhere in that general direction.

Most important of all, any solution to this problem must fulfil a number of preconditions. Specifically, it must answer each of the following questions: if any are answered wrongly, then that solution will not do.

Eustache d'Auger de Cavoye, the legendary masked man, had his face covered so that he 'would not be recognised'. Why?

Presuming, from the extremely close resemblance of his brother to the king, that Eustache also resembled Louis XIV, why did Eustache look like his monarch? Was it a coincidence or not?

And why did such a resemblance suddenly become important enough to put him in a mask when he was already almost 32 years old?

What did Eustache do in 1669 to earn his life imprisonment?

What did Eustache know, that he was to be killed instantly if he attempted to speak? What secret could be so important that security precautions had to be so extremely stringent, that his name had to be completely removed from all records, and that a cover-up had to be put into operation? What secret was not only dynastic, in that it would be a painful matter to all the Bourbon kings, but political, in that it was known to a number of ministers – including Fouquet, who probably knew it before 1661?

What was Louis XIV trying to hide in all this, that he was so obsessed with his masked prisoner? What could be so important that his own government was prompted to issue false stories and rumours that called the morals of his own family into question? Why did the king himself change so suddenly from a reserved young man into such an extravagant, authoritarian ruler?

What was the secret of the king's birth?

Why did Louis XIV, a man who could be so cruel as to sentence 349 nobles to death on a financial irregularity, not simply execute his prisoner? Why did he keep him alive? One can assume that the masked man had nothing to go back to, and that for him to try and escape would mean death, so he was better off not to complain but to stay where he was. But seeing that he was obviously never going to return to society, why did the king's officers go on to treat him with respect and deference?

Why were his mother and brother rewarded so well? Why were they so easily prepared to see Eustache go? What was the Cavoye family's part in all this?

And why was Eustache's best friend the Count of Lauzun promoted so suddenly and then arrested and imprisoned without trial? Presuming that he had betrayed Eustache, but that the king was not sure if he could subsequently be trusted himself, how was the betrayal brought about? What did Eustache tell Lauzun? And what did Lauzun think Eustache knew?

Any theory explaining the case of the man in the mask must answer these points satisfactorily. Furthermore it must fit the chronology of the case perfectly. In particular, the vital dates of his prison term from 1669 to 1703 must be observed. An answer that included all the necessary points but saw Eustache de Cavoye arrested in 1667 would not do.

There is only one outcome that can fit all these requirements satisfactorily.

20

The solution

'The great preoccupation of the monarchy had always been to safeguard the succession to the throne.' Gaxotte

Eustache d'Auger de Cavoye, third son of François d'Auger de Cavoye, the captain of Cardinal Richelieu's musketeers, was only four when his father died. But as the child moved out of infancy, he must have been aware that he was growing up into no ordinary environment. His boyhood friends were some of the highest-born in the land, including the young king himself, and his social circle was watched over carefully by Queen Anne, Cardinal Mazarin and the other ministers. Eustache must also have been aware of his mother's close connections with government; she was lady-in-waiting and close friend to the queen, as well as being great friends with Mazarin. She received a huge pension, amounting to the equivalent of £60,000, that outweighed any battlefield braveries of her dead husband and any personal influence of her own. If she needed money, a personal note from the prime minister himself to the finance minister easily fixed things up.

> Madame de Cavoye should not require any recommendation to you, but as she is very much one of my friends, I could not resist writing you these lines to inform you that it is the King's intention that she should be promptly satisfied. And I shall myself be much obliged by the care you give to the matter.

Eustache was not one to follow his allotted social path to success. He preferred to experience the wild life with his friend the Count of Lauzun. Unfortunately for everybody else concerned, Eustache's two elder brothers died by the time he was 17, so it was this untrustworthy character that succeeded them – nominally, at least – as head of the Cavoye family in 1654. It was not that he was too young to cope with such a responsibility: men had to grow up fast in the seventeenth century, and Eustache was already the veteran of two years' military campaigning. But quite simply, Eustache was a criminal in the making. The cost of his tastes outweighed his income. Left to his own devices, in fact, Eustache would probably have bankrupted the entire Cavoye family before very long. But while his mother lived she was legally entitled to restrict Eustache's annual revenue from the family estate. So Eustache fell deeper and deeper into debt, while his outrageous behaviour took him further away from the straight and narrow and deeper into a nasty underworld of poisoners, black magicians and killers who serviced the fantasies of the idle rich.

Although his mother disinherited him in 1664, as she was entitled to do, and replaced him with his younger brother Louis, Eustache had already been the titular head of his family for a decade. During that time he must have had access to the family papers. He must have begun to wonder why his mother was so influential and well off. What is clear is that whether he discovered it legally, or whether quite by chance, Eustache obviously found out some family secret of enormous significance; for when he was arrested in 1669, he was silenced forever. The authorities did not dare bring him to trial. The letters of Louvois and the king display an almost obsessive fear of Eustache talking to or communicating with anyone, with the exception of Fouquet, a minister and a relative of the Cavoyes who had already been held incommunicado since 1661. Whatever Eustache knew was an old secret, and he had probably learnt it during this period from his family.

He must have known a good number of secrets anyway.

His 'work' in the illegal drugs trade seems to have brought him into contact with various prominent figures indulging in dubious activities. But these secrets alone were not enough to merit his becoming the masked prisoner of Pignerol; others who knew such things were put on public trial in 1679, and for the most part burnt alive for their sins. Eustache's situation was more complex: whatever he had learned outweighed even the gossip of poison and black magic.

Whether or not it was known in authority that the unsavoury Eustache de Cavoye had gained possession of such important knowledge as a young man is not clear. It would probably not have mattered either way had not Louis de Cavoye, who was mainly responsible for keeping his brother's head financially above water, been taken off to the Bastille in 1668 for fighting a duel. But by the summer of 1669 Eustache was almost certainly bankrupt, with no hope of any further income to alleviate his difficulties. In this situation, in despair, it seems very likely that he decided to use what he knew to ask for financial help from the government. There was one problem: his was not an acceptable face at court. To this end he called in the Count of Lauzun to act as his go-between, no doubt in return for a slice of the proceeds.

Antoine, Count of Lauzun, probably seemed to be the ideal person to ask: he had been angling for a senior position, lost it, and there was no apparent way back for him. He was down in the doldrums. He might be reckless enough to take part in such a dangerous scheme, and he was an old friend of Eustache's. But while it is true that Lauzun was irresponsible, he was definitely not as reckless as Eustache. He had stopped well short of keeping the kind of company that Eustache had fallen into. He had never committed a serious crime, but had always restricted himself to highjinks. He probably thought that Eustache was armed only with some silly gossip about the antics of Henrietta, the king's sister-in-law, or some other mistress. We know that Eustache never told him the true secret. So the Count of Lauzun decided that Eustache was no longer worth the friendship: Lauzun betrayed his companion, in return for a better promotion than he had ever previously hoped for – to Captain of the King's Bodyguard. This was a much safer course than blackmailing the throne, an escapade which would more than likely have led them both to the scaffold. Unfortunately for Lauzun, in trying to turn the situation to his advantage, he had uncovered a hornets' nest. Not knowing the true importance of Eustache's secret, he could not know that as a matter of caution he could never be fully trusted in any political capacity again.

But what was Eustache's secret? To understand its true nature, we must go back to 1637, and the months following his own birth, to a time when Louis XIII was on the throne and Cardinal Richelieu ruled France. For Richelieu and his assistant Mazarin, everything was rosy except the future. If their king died without issue and his brother Gaston of Orléans took the throne, not only would everything they had worked for be ruined, halting the concentration of power around themselves and the eclipse of the old nobility, but – of greater urgency – they were both liable to end up without their heads. Louis XIII himself was just as keen to deny his brother, whom he disliked intensely, but under no circumstances could he bring himself to produce a child. Neither did the queen have any wish to play second fiddle to Gaston. If the king died, she wanted a son so that as regent she might control the kingdom.

At this point it is hard to believe that Richelieu would not have taken a hand. Although they liked and respected each other greatly, the king was little more than a puppet in his hands, and was willing to let the cardinal take charge. Richelieu's course was obvious. Why not bring in a surrogate father to produce an heir by the queen? It would have to be someone young, fit, healthy, intelligent, handsome, athletic, brave and utterly loyal. It would have to be someone socially acceptable and known to the king and queen, without having any claim on the throne whatsoever. It would have to be someone that nobody would suspect,

perhaps a happily married man whose wife would agree to
the scheme: certainly it would have to be a man of proven
fertility. It would have to be someone who owed everything
to the king or Cardinal Richelieu and stood to lose a great
deal if the king died and the cardinal fell, or if the secret
ever came out. And it would have to be someone who had
proven himself completely trustworthy. Who better than
Richelieu's right-hand man, his very own Captain of Musketeers, a man who had all these qualities? The same
Captain of Musketeers who was travelling with the King
and Richelieu in December 1637 when the conception of
Louis xiv took place. That Captain of Musketeers was
Eustache's father, François de Cavoye.

François fitted the bill precisely. He was a hero of the
day. He would do anything for the king and Richelieu, and
his wife Marie would do anything for the queen and
Mazarin. And he already had seven fine children of his
own. Both Louis xiii and Queen Anne knew and liked
François de Cavoye and his wife a great deal, and they
knew that they could trust them. Perhaps the king did not
take the episode as seriously as he might have done: he did,
after all, commend the provision of an heir to the Virgin
Mary and name the child 'Dieudonné', a term often used
to imply illegitimate fatherhood. But for the others involved
it was a serious matter. The French royal line descended
only through Louis, Anne herself was no part of the French
royal family, and female descent was not recognised
anyway. Between them, they were producing an heir who
had no right whatsoever to the throne: but there was
absolutely no alternative. They produced another son in
the same vein in 1640, named Philippe. Then in 1641,
François de Cavoye was killed at the siege of Bapaume.
There were no more children, and Queen Anne's mood
took on a melancholy aspect that must have bewildered her
close attendants – all, perhaps, except Marie de Cavoye.

The arrangement worked well, except that there were
two problems. The first was that Louis xiv, the young king,
bore an astonishing resemblance to the Cavoye brothers

and was completely different in every respect from Louis
XIII, whom he ignored. This at least could be laughed off as
a coincidence. But the second problem was more serious.
One of François' natural children, Eustache, by 1654 the
head of his family, must have discovered the secret of the
succession plot. And in 1669 that child, by now a spendthrift, 32-year-old wastrel, tried to put it to his own advantage. We know that Louis XIV had always tried to protect
his half-brother against his own worst excesses, but the
king's leniency only seemed to encourage Eustache. When
the Count of Lauzun came to him with news of Eustache's
plot to blackmail the throne, Louis knew that Eustache
could no longer remain at liberty. If he gave in to blackmail,
it might never end.

The arrest was easily affected. Nobody would miss such
a down-and-out because he had already dropped out of
society. Eustache was taken at Dunkirk or Calais, intending
to flee the country. Presumably Lauzun had told him of the
collapse of their plot and had arranged to meet him there.
Eustache's cell had already been prepared for him, more
than a week before he was captured by Captain Vauroy
and his group of trusted men, who had been absented from
their posts on a spurious errand. There were also some
other precautions that the king needed to take. Eustache
had to be given an assiduous watcher, the Marquis de
Louvois, who hated the Cavoyes. His name had to be
removed from the records. Louis de Cavoye, his brother,
had to be well rewarded to fend off enquiries. And in due
course Lauzun had to be spirited away – altogether a more
difficult and embarrassing proposition. Perhaps it was
feared that Lauzun knew something. Perhaps he thought
he did. Or perhaps he too pushed his luck, and asked for
yet further and further promotions in return for his silence.
Whichever the case, he too was bound for Pignerol. It made
sense to keep Eustache, Fouquet and Lauzun, the three
people who might know something about the plot, together
in the care of the same trustworthy gaoler, under the same
impregnable roof. When a fourth man was added to this

list, Fouquet's valet La Rivière, he too had to stay in the same gaol with the same gaoler.

As for Eustache, safe in his new prison, the simplest course would have been to do away with him altogether; but this man was the king's own brother. He could not be killed. Why else would a man with such a secret be kept alive? Why else would he be treated deferentially and given a relatively comfortable existence? But Eustache must never be able to tell his story to anyone. Except Fouquet – who knew already, and was trusted. His features – bearing a close resemblance to the king's – must be masked 'to avoid him being recognised'. Nobody must see a closely guarded prisoner who looked like the king and who might claim to be the king's brother. This very existence would be punishment enough for his crimes. As it was, nothing could be further from Eustache's mind than to cause another stir. As a blackmailer he was finished. Here, he had a comfortable and secure existence, with everything done for him. If he tried to talk, and make trouble, he would be killed. If he escaped, all he had to go back to was severe debt, an unsavoury array of friends who had already betrayed him once, and the knowledge that the king's assassins would never be far behind him. At first, he must have expected death. 'Does the king want my life?' he had asked St Mars. But when it became clear that his life was not in danger, why should he not be philosophical and accept his lot?

So it was that Eustache d'Auger de Cavoye came to be the man in the mask. Ultimately his gruesome punishment, while it served its purpose at the simplest level, defeated its own ends. People were more likely to ask questions about a man in a mask than about an ordinary prisoner. Rumours began to emerge from Provence about a mysterious captive who was masked because he looked like someone. It was this dilemma that led to the cover-up operation, and the 'tall stories' that were told to mislead and confuse enquirers. The alternative versions of the masked man's story that were spread by ministers and others were cleverly close to the truth. Some obliquely identified Mattioli. Others, such as that planted by Barbezieux on Madame St Quentin, identified the masked man as the illegitimate son of the queen. This is almost true – Louis XIV was. But what immediately springs to mind in this context is the child of some embarrassing liaison between the queen and a visiting duke, not surrogate royal fatherhood. Similarly, other stories told of the king's secret twin brother, a version picked up by Voltaire and Alexandre Dumas. True, he was a secret brother of the king, but not a natural brother kept secret from birth. Anyone checking the descriptions of the birth of Louis XIV would know that no twin could have been born without it becoming public knowledge.

One wonders what King Louis XIV first made of the secret that he was trying so hard to hide, that he was not the rightful king of France. Perhaps one can now understand his sudden wild urge to transform himself from a reserved young man into a glorious, extravagant and self-consciously royal figure. One wonders, also, what St Mars made of his passport to riches, his companion of thirty-four years, and whether he ever discovered the masked man's secret. If he did, he would certainly have kept quiet about the fact, so we will never know. There are so many subsidiary questions of this nature that can never be answered but only speculated upon. For instance, did Eustache have anything to do with the death of Nicolas Fouquet?

The main questions, however, have been answered. Who he was, what he knew, what he did, why it happened. How a man can apparently be arrested for possessing a secret that was several years old, and masked to conceal the same features that he had been sporting in public for thirty-two years; why people might be expected to recognise someone after thirty-four years in a cell; why a reckless courtier should be inexplicably promoted, then arrested just as incomprehensibly; why the man in the mask was never killed; and what happened to the disgraced soldier Eustache d'Auger de Cavoye in the eventful summer of 1669. We also know what Eustache knew, and must have ruefully reflected upon in his prison: that the king of France, and all the kings that succeeded him, were no more the rightful kings of France than was the gaoler who brought the prisoner his dinner every day.

Appendix

Lauzun in Ireland

The Count of Lauzun was released in 1681 – still convinced of his innocence after ten years in gaol – after court pressure from his friends and from his fiancée, the King's cousin, Mademoiselle de Montpensier; and perhaps also as a result of Fouquet's evidence. Following a lengthy interview with Louvois and the King, he was reinstated under house arrest with a personal guard, some distance from Paris. Eventually, however, he was allowed to lead a military expedition to Ireland – no doubt the French equivalent of the Eastern front – where he was captured by the British. His personal papers were taken at the same time, and they contained a number of messages in code from Louvois. The Earl of Nottingham commanded John Wallis to decipher the captured letters as quickly as possible, 'they seeming to containe matters of great importance'. But Wallis was forced to reply to the Earl that he had never mastered any of Louvois' ciphers. It is almost certain that these messages relate only to the war against Britain, but as they have never been decoded to this day, it is just possible that they have some bearing on the events in this book.

For the benefit of anyone interested in decoding them, the following is a substantial extract from one of the letters. The others are contained in the British Museum.

Letter from Louvois to Lauzun 27 May 1690

Monsieur,
J'accuserais par cette lettre la reception de celles que vous m'avez

fait l'honneur de m'escrire les 3eme, 5eme, 12eme, 16eme, et 25eme du mois passé. 1er, 4eme, et 18eme du courant desquelles le Roy a entendu la lecture avec plaisir et a fort loué tout ceque vous avez fait tant a Cork que depuis que vous estes arrivé pres du Roy d'Angleterre. Sa Ma(jes)te a fort approuvé le compte que vous luy en rendez, Et m'a Commandé de vous fait sçavoir qu'elle en estoit tres satisfaite et vous recommandoit de continuer a en(voyer) sa (Majesté) tousjours de mesme 176. 134. 89. 65. 132. 34. 3. 200. 84. 379. 360. 281. 140. 26. 366. 262. 102. 192. 79. 76. 291. 15. 37. 297. 110. 243. 45. 401. 422. 317. 121. 69. 205. 26. 23. 221. 143. 303. 359. 88. 156. 79. 4. 41. 275. 403. 409. 237. 97. 316. 406. 216. 383. 180. 65. 395. 40. 421. 7. 216. 310. 381. 375. 244. 433. 222. 39. 419. 173. 132. 146. 340. 65. 385. 196.

Je vous suplie de m'envoyer des memoires apart qui me marquent quelles charges vous avez remplies dans l'infanterie, Et les noms et (?) de ceux a qui vous les avez données. 290. 225. 23. 372. 298. 185. 348. 144. 13. 123. 59. 79. 340. 316. 261. 277. 201. 184. 339. 107. 298. 39. 131. 156. 4. 344. 400. 65. 338. 69. 89. 121. 373. 416. 205. 372. 297. 344. 95. 156. 219. 230. 303. 33. 96. 57. 417. 348. 390. 143. 261. 3. 123. 243. 339. 383. 157. 89. 344. 296. 287. 316. 79. 17. 140. 448. 390. 112. 105. 253. 203. 205. 375. 52. 223. 84. 210. 135. 237. 110. 137. 75. 45. 322. 361. 232. 10. 223. 123. 321. 157. 178. 59. 418. 311. 61. 312. 205. 338. 73. 247. 15. 139. 297. 107. 298. 390. 419. 10. 278. 185. 79. 446. 37. 89. 13. 39. 157. 379. 149. 144. 13. 123. 348. 121. 340. 7. 68. 61. 102, 278. 47. 339. 261. 69. 339. 447. 301. 208. 168. 158. 416. 344. 287. 204. 372. 96. 112. 200. 230. 115. 33. 45. 398. 372. 40. 493. 144. 124. 131. 173. 210. 272. 72. 51. 280. 179. 76. 121. 97. 148. 7. 79. 47. 132. 186. 426. 61. 297. 2. 121. 438. 381. 13. 124. 337. 322. 290. 101. 261. 79. 373. 244. 205. 143. 384. 84. 243. 45. 76. 340. 65. 4. 143. 450. 375. 400. 132. 440. 4. 210. 173. 433. 37. 15. 232. 131. 211. 208. 140. 121. 337. 139. 297. 204. 1. 59. 345. 157. 178. 26. 359. 256. 40. 88. 344. 416. 47. 243. 201. 137. 140. 65. 88. 232. 370. 281. 37. 244. 61. 258. 73. 303. 179. 102. 203. 443. 299. 433. 33. 381. 71. 114. 259. 57. 203. 2. 417. 230. 390. 264. 105. 79. 294. 314. 438. 132. 65. 158. 384. 59. 253. 203. 392. 381. 223. 230. 332. 143. 258. 5. 426. 140. 196. 253. 203. 398. 348. 34. 337. 88. 59. 208. 290. 134. 89. 65. 433. 34. 3. 200. 84. 17. 274. 360. 281. 297. 262. 278. 156. 237. 135. 15. 110. 137. 75. 45. 157. 143. 281. 61. 108. 39. 139. 146. 65. 2. 99. 40. 401. 232. 430. 37. 250. 228. 131. 12. 132. 146. 359. 81. 223. 348.

210. 360. 400. 398. 23. 203. 167. 141. 157. 298. 84. 344. 296. 107.
59. 85. 315. 403. 409. 68. 398. 183. 176. 30.

Le Roy ayant apris la mort de Mons(ieur) d'Escotre a donné a
son fils le Regiment qu'il avoit et la lieutenance de Roy de Brie
dont il estoit pourvue, Et Sa Ma(jes)te a en mesme temps fait
Brigadier Mons(ieur) de Zurlauben, Je vous envoye les ordres du
Roy necessaires pour le faire reconnoistre, Sa Ma(jes)te n'ayant
pas crû qu'il fust de sa justice de luy preferer Mr de Merode qui
n'est entré a son service que depuis deux and etauparavant n'avoit
servy que de volontaire.

176. 90. 101. 102. 372. 23. 429. 253. 185. 201. 250. 97. 380. 79.
157. 261. 359. 201. 379. 412. 59. 196. 45. 69. 135. 109. 37. 99. 237.
384. 14. 17. 401. 40. 165. 230. 421. 139. 4. 446. 180. 99. 398. 344.
52. 122. 249. 438. 221. 76. 129. 128. 33. 419. 376. 478. 390. 157.
47. 132. 186. 433. 264. 73. 95. 179. 253. 203. 414. 191. 311. 205.
114. 137. 103. 225. 196. 39. 240. 372. 226. 84. 37. 88. 208. 299.
337. 238. 243. 156. 315. 15. 200. 340. 65. 278. 426. 88. 203. 114.
234. 196. 421. 65. 293. 399. 84. 135. 45. 417. 292. 414. 294. 204.
193. 368. 61. 446. 157. 332. 97. 433. 208. 208. 143. 144. 7. 121.
108. 173. 200. 40. 381. 2. 221. 230. 253. 203. 87. 69. 288. 318. 68.
132. 132. 65. 47. 135. 253. 203. 392. 359. 112. 140. 406. 122. 303.
205. 71. 143. 393. 65. 23. 203. 233. 101. 89. 204. 287. 88. 144. 280.
154. 243. 139. 297. 281. 81. 282. 137. 157. 261. 388. 121. 184. 135.
250. 6. 322. 30. 438. 416. 99. 401. 392. 238. 209. 368. 61. 446. 37.
178. 89. 78. 47. 862. 256. 348. 39. 419. 115. 143. 421. 302. 418. 79.
180. 417. 398. 190. 40. 294. 112. 105. 4. 33. 68. 174. 439. 148. 273.
6. 37. 178. 209. 121. 244. 65. 447. 95. 118. 179. 337. 141. 426. 135.
89. 61. 281. 392. 47. 243. 297. 73. 389. 375. 278. 303. 192. 33. 205.
118. 40. 143. 409. 68. 398. 359. 190. 84. 2. 94. [or 294.] 375. 400.
13. 39. 258. 105. 30. 410. 101. 359. 80. 398. 348. 414. 214. 59. 230.
37. 225. 65. 344. 52. 316. 200. 404. 240. 61. 360. 196. 143. 108.
303. 210. 121. 180. 398. 61. 323. 341. 373. 264. 396. 26. 140. 61.
108. 3. 168. 434. 173. 15. 262. 69. 286. 26. 225. 413. 341. 370. 79.
101. 57. 406. 122. 400. 131. 157. 261. 331. 17. 129. 40. 433. 447.
97. 81. 84. 132. 260. 208. 167. 207. 381. 135. 94. 52. 123. 390. 144.
262. 1. 348. 368. 156. 230. 96. 205. 108. 4. 210. 79. 426. 180. 99.
321. 7. 121. 192. 65. 127. 76. 412. 198. 27. 65. 89. 326. 433. 360.
81. 137. 140. 337. 398. 392. 47. 237. 201. 244. 419. 173. 326. 57.
124. 370. 85. 237. 384. 297. 411. 290. 56. 225. 102. 372. 23. 209.
253. 278. 201. 157. 261. 44. 221. 59. 17. 310. 108. 439. 285. 19. 39.

7. 143. 344. 150. 107. 426. 205. 204. 316. 121. 100. 79. 200. 84.
135. 258. 73. 400. 179. 243. 144. 39. 119. 203. 96. 241. 132. 428.
41. 421. 259. 418. 173. 33. 101. 89. 121. 373. 95. 297. 205. 65. 360.
409. 291. 280. 348. 39. 135. 84. 150. 53. 337. 112. 105. 4. 37. 301.
108. 164. 238. 316. 426. 65. 108. 58. 216. 2. 417. 40. 379. 61. 301.
365. 296. 221. 59. 157. 250. 5. 297. 312.
Le Roy trouve bon que le S(ieur) Soulegre reste en irlande
pourvue qu'il vous donne lieu d'estre satisfait de sa conduite.

Monsieur.
V(otr)e tres humble et tres affectioné serviteur
　　　　　　　　　　　　　　　M. Louvois

NICHOLAS HARMAN

DUNKIRK: THE NECESSARY MYTH

'In this first-class historical account, Nicholas Harman seeks to kill some of the myths which are popularly associated with the evacuation of May 1940. With skill and admirable research, he reveals how the British deliberately duped the French, letting them hold the Dunkirk perimeter while the BEF escaped'   *The Daily Telegraph*

For forty years Dunkirk has been celebrated as one of Britain's greatest triumphs – the incredible operation that saved 340,000 British soldiers from death or capture. But, in this major new book, the author argues that the Dunkirk spirit was to a considerable extent based on myth; and that behind the bravery and the faith there was also deception and trickery, conflict and contradictory orders at the political and high command level.

'An enthralling account of those thrilling events in the summer of 1940'   *Yorkshire Post*

Post·A·Book

A Royal Mail service in association with the Book Marketing Council & The Booksellers Association.
Post-A-Book is a Post Office trademark.

MICHAEL LEWIS

LIAR'S POKER

'An amazing book, readable, funny and mind-boggling . . . one of the great business books of all time'   *Punch*

'If you thought Gordon Gekko of the *Wall Street* movie was an implausibly corrupt piece of fiction, see how you like the real thing. This rip-the-lid-off account of the bond-dealing brouhaha is the work of a real-life bond salesman . . . Read all about it; headlong greed, inarticulate obscenity, *Animal House* horseplay . . .'   *The Sunday Times*

From mere trainee to lowly geek, to triumphal Big Swinging Dick: that was Michael Lewis' pell-mell progress through the dealing rooms of Salomon Brothers in New York and London during the heady mid-1980s when they were probably the world's most powerful and profitable merchant bank.

A true-life *Bonfire of the Vanities*, funny, frightening, breathless and heartless, his is a tale of hysterical greed and ambition set in an obsessed, enclosed world . . .

'Immense verve and wit'   *20/20 Magazine*

'Should be made a legally required component of every MBA course'   *Management Today*

'As traders would say, this book is a buy'   *Financial Times*

'A highly immoral book'   *Daily Mail*

'Wickedly funny'   *Daily Express*

HODDER AND STOUGHTON PAPERBACKS

PAT MOLLOY

THE CANNOCK CHASE MURDERS

In January 1966, the sexually-assaulted bodies of two little girls were discovered on Cannock Chase, north of Birmingham. Seventeen months later, a third small child was abducted and murdered.

The search for the Cannock Chase murderer was to become the biggest child-murder hunt ever, lasting four years.

The then Detective Sergeant Pat Molloy, who was involved throughout, has written a fascinating insider's account of the investigation. How it feels to work on a murder hunt for twelve hours or more a day, seven days a week, for months on end. How the relevant information has to be sorted out of literally tons of paperwork; of the false hopes, the disappointments, the domestic disruption; the mistakes and the lessons learned.

The Cannock Chase Murders takes you unforgettably to the very heart of a major police operation.

HODDER AND STOUGHTON PAPERBACKS

OTHER NON-FICTION TITLES AVAILABLE FROM HODDER AND STOUGHTON PAPERBACKS

	NICHOLAS HARMAN	
☐ 51785 9	Dunkirk: The Neccessary Myth	£4.50
	RICHARD HOUGH AND DENIS RICHARDS	
☐ 53470 2	The Battle of Britain	£4.99
	MICHAEL LEWIS	
☐ 53469 9	Liar's Poker	£3.99
	PAT MALLOY	
☐52089 2	The Cannock Chase Murders	£3.99
	STERLING SEAGRAVE	
☐ 53082 5	The Marcos Dynasty	£5.99
☐ 39511 1	The Soong Dynasty	£5.95

All these books are available at your local bookshop or newsagent, or can be ordered direct from the publisher. Just tick the titles you want and fill in the form below.

Prices and availability subject to change without notice.

HODDER AND STOUGHTON PAPERBACKS, P.O. Box 11, Falmouth, Cornwall.

Please send cheque or postal order, and allow the following for postage and packing:

U.K. – 80p for one book, plus 20p for each additional book ordered up to a £2.00 maximum.

B.F.P.O. – 80p for the first book, plus 20p for each additional book.

OVERSEAS INCLUDING EIRE – £1.50 for the first book, plus £1.00 for second book, and 30p for each additional book ordered.

NAME ....

ADDRESS ....

....